The United States and the Multilateral Development Banks

The United States and the Multilateral Development Banks

A Report of the CSIS Task Force on the Multilateral Development Banks.

Project Cochairs

Senator Bill Bradley
Representative John R. Kasich

Project Director

Barbara Upton

March 1998

About CSIS

The Center for Strategic and International Studies (CSIS), established in 1962, is a private, tax-exempt institution focusing on international public policy issues. Its research is nonpartisan and nonproprietary.

CSIS is dedicated to policy impact. It seeks to inform and shape selected policy decisions in government and the private sector to meet the increasingly complex and difficult global challenges that leaders will confront in the next century. It achieves this mission in three ways: by generating strategic analysis that is anticipatory and interdisciplinary; by convening policymakers and other influential parties to assess key issues; and by building structures for policy action.

CSIS does not take specific public policy positions. Accordingly, all views, positions, and conclusions expressed in this publication should be understood to be solely those of the authors.

Library of Congress Cataloging-in-Publication Data
CIP information available upon request

©1998 by The Center for Strategic and International Studies
All rights reserved.
ISBN: 0-89206-326-2

The CSIS Press
Center for Strategic and International Studies
1800 K Street, NW, Washington, DC 20006
Telephone: (202) 887-0200; Fax: (202) 775-3199
E-mail: books@csis.org
Web site: http://www.csis.org/

Contents

Acknowledgments   vii

Task Force Members   x

Executive Summary   1

1. Introduction   17

2. Conclusions   23

3. Recommendations   36

    Access to MDB Resources   36

    Use of MDB Resources   43

    MDB Operations   63

    Evaluating Performance of the MDBs   87

    U.S. Financial Support   93

    Implementation of Recommendations   97

Appendix A. U.S. Funding of the MDBs   99

Appendix B. Existing MDB Programs in Support of
             Private Projects   102

Appendix C. Partnerships to Expand MDB Capacity   104

Appendix D. Examples of Discrepancies between
             MDB Policies and Performance   108

Appendix E. Examination of New MDB Replenishment
             Agreements   113

Appendix F. Background Papers Prepared for the Task Force   125

Appendix G. Additional Statements of Task Force Members   131

Appendix H. Statement by Senator Joseph R. Biden   152

Acknowledgments

After the fiftieth anniversary of the founding of the World Bank in 1994, the controversy surrounding whether the World Bank and its four regional bank siblings (the Inter-American Development Bank [IDB], the Asian Development Bank [ADB], the African Development Bank [AfDB], and the European Bank for Reconstruction and Development [EBRD]) were still important priorities for the United States appeared to deepen. Articles appeared advocating privatization of the World Bank, a worldwide nongovernmental organization (NGO) consortium said "50 years is enough," and a newly elected U.S. Congress drastically cut budget requests for the five multilateral development banks (MDBs).

In early 1996, the Center for Strategic and International Studies (CSIS) constituted its bipartisan Task Force on the United States and the MDBs chaired by Senator Bill Bradley and Representative John Kasich. Its aim was to take a fresh look at whether from the U.S. perspective the MDBs were still needed; if so, for what functions, and were they performing those functions effectively. A major effort was made to include in the Task Force representatives of all U.S. groups with an interest in the MDBs, people with knowledge of the many facets of the institutions' work, and individuals with both critical and supportive initial views.

The group met as a whole 3 times and in open working groups on various topics about 20 times. Two of the general meetings were chaired by Lawrence Ricciardi, senior vice president and general counsel of the IBM Corporation, who brought to bear his depth of experience from both private- and public-sector perspectives in international development issues.

In addition to Task Force members, many individuals and groups generously supported this effort with their knowledge and views. Wayne Struble and Linda Menghetti, from the staffs of Representative Kasich and Senator Bradley, respectively, devoted innumerable hours to the Task Force's work and were instrumental at every step of the process, as was Douglas Worth of the IBM Corporation. At CSIS, Ambassador Ernest Preeg, who chaired the Working Group on Private Sector Development, as well as David Wendt and John Yochelson made valuable contributions based on long and relevant experience in their fields.

Laura Foose, Karen Levy, Lisa Hyland, Krishnan Chettur, Geoffrey Davis, and Zach Gast coordinated various aspects of the project and provided substantive input in their areas.

Finally, many individuals in all five MDBs made available their time and points of view, especially Richard Frank, Alexander Shakow, and Judith Maguire in the World Bank, Nicholas Stern in the EBRD, Shoji Nishimoto, Arun Adarkar, and Ronda Bresnick in the ADB, Delphin Rwegasira and G. M. Woldu in the AfDB, and Stephen Quick, William Robinson, and Nan Burroughs in the IDB.

Unlike many large groups looking at complex issues whose work often ends with a chair's summary of discussions or a short list of general conclusions, this Task Force produced a comparatively lengthy set of conclusions and recommendations. It did this, at the cost of extra time for all concerned, out of a belief that in many cases short generalizations would not do justice to the multifaceted issues and nuanced judgments involved and could further obscure a debate that has already been clouded by too much rhetoric that is not substantiated by specific actions and evidence. The group thought it was not sufficient to say that the MDBs should be more effective; it was necessary to specify in what ways they should become more effective and how an outsider could reach reasonable conclusions about whether they had done so.

The conclusions and recommendations represent the views of the Task Force as modified by the additional statements of some members included in Appendix G. Some original members did not sign the final report (their names are not included) for reasons ranging from lack of time to consider it fully to substantive disagreements with the thrust of the report. On several issues where the group was divided, it was decided to present options and report the percentage of Task Force members favoring each option (Recommendations 6 and 17–18).

Barbara Upton
Project Director
United States and the MDBs Project
December 1997

The Task Force gratefully acknowledges the financial support of:

The Ford Foundation

IBM

AES Corporation

Citibank N.A.

Cravath, Swaine & Moore

Davis Polk & Wardwell

Destec Energy

Entergy Enterprises

F. C. Schaffer and Associates

Goldman Sachs International

Lehman Brothers

Morgan Stanley

NationsBank

Raytheon Engineers and Constructors

The Reader's Digest Association

U S WEST

Western States Machine Company

Task Force Members

Project Cochairs

Senator Bill Bradley

> Linda Menghetti, *Legislative Assistant*

Representative John R. Kasich

> Wayne T. Struble, *Staff Director, House Budget Committee*

Other Members of Congress*

Representative Charles F. Bass

> Matthew L. Vaughan, *Legislative Director*

Representative Floyd H. Flake

> Sean Peterson, *Chief of Staff*

Representative Benjamin A. Gilman

> Mark Kirk, *Counsel*

Representative Tony P. Hall

> Kimberly A. Miller, *Legislative Assistant*

Representative James A. Leach

> James McCormick, *Assistant Staff Director, House Committee on Banking and Financial Services*

Representative Constance A. Morella

> Mickie B. Reed, *Legislative Assistant*
>
> Craig S. Powers, *Legislative Assistant*

Senator Carol Moseley-Braun

> Chailendu Pegues, *Legislative Assistant*
>
> Kellie Larkin, *Legislative Assistant*
>
> Anne Ruhle, *Legislative Assistant*

Other Task Force Members

Nancy Alexander
Program Manager, Development Bank Watchers' Project, Bread for the World Institute

George B. N. Ayittey
Associate Professor of Economics, American University

Douglas Bandow
Senior Fellow, Cato Institute
former Special Assistant to President Reagan

David D. Bathrick
former President, Association for International Agriculture and Rural Development
former Director of Agricultural Programs, U.S. Agency for International Development

---

* Senator Joseph R. Biden, who became ranking minority member on the Senate Foreign Relations Committee in January 1997, was not a member of the Task Force but supports the efforts of the Task Force as noted in his letter on page 152.

John Bohn
*former U.S. Executive Director, Asian
Development Bank
former President, Export-Import Bank
former President, Moodys Investors Service*

Barbara J. Bramble
*Director, International Office, National
Wildlife Federation*

Robert Browne
*former U.S. Executive Director, African
Development Bank
former Staff Director, Subcommittee on
Domestic and International Monetary
Policy, House Banking Committee*

James B. Burnham
*former U.S. Executive Director, World Bank
Murrin Professor of Global Competitiveness,
Duquesne University*

Irvin D. Coker
*former Deputy Assistant Secretary, Department
of Health, Education, and Welfare
former Mission Director to Ghana and
Uganda, U.S. Agency for International
Development*

Lew Cramer
*Vice President for Federal Relations, U S
WEST*

Nicholas Eberstadt
*American Enterprise Institute
Harvard Center for Population and
Development Studies*

Hilary F. French
*Vice President for Research, Worldwatch
Institute*

Bryant George
*former Ford Foundation Representative
Microcredit Consultant to the Government of
South Africa*

Jo Marie Griesgraber
*Project Director, Rethinking Bretton Woods,
Center of Concern*

Catherine Gwin
*Senior Vice President, Overseas Development
Council*

Lara Helfer
*formerly with Program on International
Financial and Development Institutions,
International Institute for Energy
Conservation*

Henrietta Holsman Fore
Chair, Holsman International

Marshall Kaplan
*Dean and Professor of Public Policy, Graduate
School of Public Affairs, University of
Colorado at Denver*

Gregory D. Kingsley
Director, Project Finance, Destec Energy

James Kunder
*former Vice President for Program
Development, Save the Children
Federation*

Allan H. Meltzer
*University Professor of Political Economy and
Public Policy, Graduate School of
Industrial Administration, Carnegie
Mellon University
American Enterprise Institute*

John Mullen
*former President, Romanian-American
Enterprise Fund
former Deputy General Counsel and Assistant
Administrator for Private Enterprise, U.S.
Agency for International Development*

Mima S. Nedelcovych
*former U.S. Executive Director, African
Development Bank
Vice President, International Business
Development, F. C. Schaffer and
Associates, Inc.*

Seamus O'Cleireacain
*Professor, Purchase College, State University
of New York
Carnegie Endowment for International Peace*

Anne Predieri
Director, NationsBank Capital Markets, Inc.

Ernest Preeg
*William M. Scholl Chair in International
   Business, Center for Strategic and
   International Studies*

Kevin F. F. Quigley
*Vice President, Contemporary Affairs and
   Corporate Programs, Asia Society*

Gustav Ranis
*Director, Yale Center for International and
   Area Studies*
*Frank Altschul Professor of International
   Economics, Yale University*

Dr. Musunuru S. Rao
*former Manager, Social Development Division,
   Asian Development Bank*

L. R. Ricciardi
*Senior Vice President and General Counsel,
   IBM Corporation*

Bruce Rich
*Director, International Program,
   Environmental Defense Fund*

Theodore Roosevelt IV
Managing Director, Lehman Brothers

Donald C. Roth
*Managing Director, Emerging Markets
   Partnership*

Frances Seymour
*Director, Development Assistance Policy,
   World Wildlife Fund*

James Sheehan
*Research Associate, Competitiveness
   Enterprise Institute*

D. E. Smee
*Senior Adviser for International Operations,
   Citibank, N.A.*

Abelardo L. Valdez
Attorney at Law
former Ambassador
*former Assistant Administrator, U.S. Agency
   for International Development*

Ian Vasquez
*Director of Global Liberties Project, Cato
   Institute*

Sidney Weintraub
*William E. Simon Chair in Political Economy,
   Center for Strategic and International
   Studies*

Lawrence Yanovitch
*Director, Policy and Research, FINCA
   International*

Dennis T. Yasutomo
Professor of Government, Smith College

Executive Summary

The MDBs Face a Changed World

The arena in which the five multilateral development banks (MDBs) operate has changed almost beyond recognition since they were founded and even since the last public assessment of U.S. participation in the MDBs was concluded in 1982. The Cold War is over, as is the consensus among the United States and its allies on bolstering politically like-minded nations through MDB and bilateral aid flows for security reasons, regardless of the recipients' economic policy performance. Also, national economic strategies throughout the world have shifted toward market approaches; as a result of this, and increasing sophistication about opportunities in developing countries, private capital flows to these countries have increased five-fold from 1990 to 1996, to over 16 times the net flows of the MDBs. Private flows are highly concentrated in 12 mostly large countries, however.

While these changes were occurring and as global economic output increased fivefold from 1950 to 1990, total world population doubled and so did the number of people living in absolute poverty. Also, many people became concerned about damage to the environment, the rapid increase in the use of natural resources, and the harm this could bring to their quality of life.

Finally, problems with deficits and debt have led both developed and developing nations to set higher standards for public-sector expenditures and the United States to question the effectiveness of international aid, including U.S. contributions to the MDBs.

MDB Objectives Remain Important U.S. Interests

In spite of these changes, the objectives of the MDBs of reducing poverty, stimulating broad-based economic growth, and promoting environmental sustainability continue to be important U.S. interests. They are prerequisites to reducing political and social instability, which, if left unchecked, has enormous security, economic, and social costs for both the United States and the developing world. If achieved, the MDBs' objectives will provide a powerful stimulus for international economic growth and significant trade and commercial opportunities for the United States. However, recent changes have significantly affected what the MDBs are needed to do to move toward these objectives.

Traditional Roles of the MDBs Should Be Modified

Since their inception, the MDBs have taken on a number of roles—as bankers, as aid agencies, as consulting firms, and as purveyors of leverage to induce policy reforms. Recent developments call for changes in these roles:

❑ The MDBs' financial intermediation or banking function—channeling funds to potentially financially viable projects and creditworthy countries—is needed in fewer countries, sectors, and projects in view of the development of private capital markets. Hence, the MDBs should substantially upgrade their ability and willingness to target their resource transfers to fewer countries and projects where they are still needed, but where policy conditions prevail that will permit the achievement of program objectives.

❑ The MDBs' aid function—channeling resources to uncreditworthy countries and to projects that have potentially high social, economic, and environmental returns but cannot attract private funding—has come under severe pressure to demonstrate effectiveness. Substantial experience shows that development cannot be induced by resource transfers alone, but depends heavily on appropriate policies, functioning institutions, and cohesive societies. The standard MDB product of large loans to a borrowing government made by a distant MDB is not suitable for some borrowers and important types of activities.

❑ The MDBs' technical advice function faces competition as the growth of global consulting firms and technological advances make world-class technical knowledge more readily obtainable from a variety of sources. Evidence suggests, however, that sometimes MDB programs suffer from a lack of sufficient knowledge of local situations. Therefore, the MDBs need to fine-tune their "knowledge" product to avoid duplicating what is available elsewhere and add more capability to acquire knowledge of local situations.

❑ Experience has shown the limits of the MDBs' ability to exert leverage for policy changes. If policy reforms are not based on genuine borrower conviction and local choices, they are unlikely to be consistently and successfully implemented. Therefore, the MDBs' role in supplying financing to support policy change should be carried out with greater discernment and selectivity.

❑ The MDBs' ability to convene or bring together diverse groups both within countries and among countries to address common problems may have been underestimated and perhaps underutilized.

MDBs Have Strengths and Weaknesses That Help and Hinder Them in Making Changes

The MDBs benefit from their relatively cost-effective means of raising funds by sharing funding requirements broadly among countries and tapping capital markets cheaply. Most of them have accumulated significant financial capital and intellectual talent. They can also build on their established roles as leaders in the international economic system, clearinghouses for useful information, and sources of policy advice, all of which are facilitated by their multinational character and their historic role.

The MDBs also have weaknesses, however, many of which were caused by their shareholders, including the United States. The first is their tendency to acquire a proliferation of functions without resolving conflicts among them, setting priorities, relinquishing unsuitable roles, or in some cases realistically facing the changes that will be needed in their operations if they are to perform new functions well. This problem often is caused by an inability to resolve differences among shareholders.

In some areas the MDBs also have accumulated outdated and inflexible structures. Some have become large, change-resistant bureaucracies that are adept at keeping outsiders from differentiating between public-relations pronouncements and real changes in bank activities.

Finally, deeply ingrained incentives apparently impel the banks to place top priority on large-scale lending and activities that facilitate such lending, even when current needs call for the banks' role to be much more differentiated and complex. This problem was clearly and publicly identified in 1992 (when the World Bank did its Portfolio Management Task Force Report and the regional banks followed with similar studies), but appears to resist solution.

U.S. Policy

The United States should have a clear vision of the role it wants the MDBs to play and support a well-defined set of policy changes and structural reforms within the institutions to support that vision. Institutions like the MDBs and pursuing their objectives are still very much needed. The question is whether these institutions can make the reforms needed to fulfill their objectives in today's environment.

In pressing a specific and significant reform agenda, the United States can draw on its ability to exercise leadership in these institutions disproportionate to its funding, which is derived from its historic role and associated privileges (e.g., naming the president of the World Bank) and from its world leadership role.

If the United States presses the agenda recommended by this Task Force, it should be helped by the fact that these recommendations do not reflect a narrow U.S. perspective. The Task Force strongly believes that these recommendations are as much in the interests of citizens of the borrowing countries and taxpayers in other donor countries as they are in those of the United States. They are not intended to secure advantages for U.S. individuals or firms, and reflect only the most broad political motivations.

As the United States pursues its policy vision, in view of the opaque nature of the institutions and the difficulty of ascertaining whether policy changes have been made operational, U.S. policy recommendations should be translated into monitorable steps so that all U.S. stakeholders can follow progress. All Task Force recommendations are accompanied by a specific "benchmark," which is one way by which progress toward the group's suggestions might be tracked.

U.S. Financial Support

Spending for the MDBs should provide results and benefits that, although indirect for U.S. citizens, equal results and benefits from other types of government spending. If the MDBs can make substantial progress toward their objectives, they are priority uses of U.S. resources. Their ability to do this, however, varies by bank and depends on their ability to focus attention on currently needed functions and to improve effectiveness. They also need more systematic, rigorous, and transparent means for shareholders to evaluate the results of their work.

A sizable majority of the Task Force rejected the view that the MDBs are no longer needed or already have sufficient resources to perform needed functions, and therefore the United States should make no new contributions. Likewise, a sizable majority rejected the idea that the MDBs so strongly serve U.S. foreign policy or commercial interests that U.S. funding should necessarily remain constant into the future for all the institutions at previously negotiated levels adjusted for inflation.

Instead, most Task Force members believe that the extent to which the MDBs are in the U.S. interest depends on their performance in important areas and that at some point the United States should link its level of financial support to the performance of each MDB. (See Option 3 on page 94.)

The Task Force had two points of view about how soon the United States should specifically look to progress toward reforms recommended to influence U.S. annual appropriations. One group (75 percent) thought the banks should not be held accountable for reforms such as those suggested below until future funding replenishments are negotiated, while the other (approximately 25 percent) believed it is reasonable to take account of progress toward these reforms as early as the next fiscal year's budget. (See Variations 1 and 2 on page 96.)

Changing Role of the Banks

Who Gets Resources

In looking at changes needed in the MDBs, the Task Force concluded that access to MDB resources should be limited to

❏ Countries making a significant effort to help their own people

The MDBs should lend only to countries that are maintaining a policy framework adequate to achieve economically, environmentally, and socially sustainable growth. This requirement that MDB borrowers be pursuing sound economic, poverty reduction, and environmental policies is different from that used by most of the MDBs now because it calls for a determination that a country's policies are adequate to be the first factor considered, rather than just one of a number of criteria. A second difference is that commitment to poverty reduction and sound environmental stewardship is included equally in the standard for policy adequacy, because major policy failures in any of these areas will undermine prospects for broadly shared, sustained development. (See Recommendation 1 on page 39.)

❏ Countries where governance is adequate to permit program success

The MDBs should more actively support improved governance as a means to achieve economic growth and poverty reduction, including by only lending to countries whose quality of governance is adequate for the success of MDB programs. (See Recommendation 2 on page 41.)

❏ Countries not yet able to mobilize sufficient private or domestic funds

Each MDB should have clear criteria by which countries that are making significant economic progress and are now able to mobilize more domestic resources and private funds graduate from its lending facilities. They also should have active programs to implement and update graduation policies. (See Recommendation 3 on page 42.)

Use of Resources

The job of the MDBs has become more difficult. They must distinguish among situations and countries to take account of where their standard products do not work or are no longer needed. They also must devise new vehicles and modalities where their traditional ones have not been successful. Often the problems that they will still be needed to address will be the toughest ones, those where public and private interests conflict or those that the private sector has not been able to solve.

The MDBs' unique qualities as multilateral public-sector institutions, which can link conceptual work with funding, can be very useful, but targeting those skills where they are still needed and showing that they can achieve results against these challenges will not be easy. In using their resources the MDBs should

❏ Use fast-disbursing policy-based lending more selectively

Many MDBs have made fast-disbursing policy-based loans in situations where insufficient local dialogue and commitment resulted in poor implementation. The MDBs should make this type of loan only in the rarer instances in which a comprehensive package of reforms with broad local support is put forward by a reforming government. Loan disbursement should be directly linked to reform implementation. This more discerning and rigorous approach should also apply to sector-specific policy-based loans. (See Recommendation 4 on page 43 and Recommendation 8c on page 63.)

❑ Adopt clearer measures to avoid competing with the private sector in infrastructure and productive sectors

The MDBs (except for the European Bank for Reconstruction and Development) have not responded consistently and transparently to the rapid expansion in the availability of private funds for infrastructure and large-scale productive projects. This dramatic and ongoing change in the reach of global capital markets requires much clearer policies and transparent procedures to ensure that the banks do not displace available private funding or fund projects that the private sector would finance if borrowing governments adopted needed policy reforms. Exceptions would be cases where market failures or externalities make private funding impractical or undesirable. (See Recommendation 5 on page 45.)

❑ Place more emphasis on developing the institutional, regulatory, and policy framework for private-sector development

The MDBs as multilateral public-sector institutions are in a unique position to urge and help borrowers to develop the institutions, regulations, and policy framework both to facilitate private-sector development and to safeguard public interests from corrupt distortions of it. The MDBs should broaden the range of business practice issues they deal with and exert more proactive leadership on a wider range of regulatory issues, from environmental and safety issues to competition policy. They also need to change their operational practices and differentiate their product line so they can give priority attention to products such as institutional development, leadership, and policy advice that may not be linked to large loans. (See the discussion of the private sector beginning on page 29.)

❑ Direct MDB support for private projects

- Task Force members had differing views on the extent to which the MDBs should provide direct support to projects involving private investment, through guarantees, loans, equity, and political-risk insurance.

  17 percent supported maintenance of the current level and type of MDB programs to assist private transactions.

  11 percent supported abolishing MDB programs that directly support private projects.

  27 percent supported a revised and somewhat expanded program of bank support for private projects. This would include stronger up-front policy conditions and a rapid and clearly defined phaseout plan. An additional 13 percent supported a variant of this option calling for a small expansion in private programs over a longer time horizon.

33 percent endorsed a larger expansion in bank support for private projects with a longer phaseout period and a larger share of funding going to private transactions. (See Recommendation 6b on page 49.)

- The MDBs should select private projects for support on the basis of expected contribution to the country's overall development objectives. (See Recommendation 6a on page 48.)

- The Task Force thought that either expanded or current level private-sector programs could be advanced with greater efficiency in the World Bank Group if a decision were made either to focus responsibility for private-sector projects in the Bank itself, after removing the charter requirement for a government guarantee, or to clearly establish IFC/ MIGA as the private transaction center. (See Recommendation 6c on page 52.)

❏ Poverty reduction: focus on borrower commitment to broadly shared growth, productive projects, and new modalities

- Sustainable poverty reduction must be based on borrower policies that will lead to broadly shared economic growth. In countries committed to this objective, the MDBs can provide policy advice on difficult issues and help examine country programs for effectiveness in benefiting needy groups. When this local commitment is lacking, MDB efforts to support poverty reduction are likely to have benefits diverted and not lead to sustainable opportunities for the poor. Humanitarian aid agencies with grant resources can ameliorate human suffering in these circumstances. (See Recommendation 7 on page 54.)

- Direct MDB poverty reduction efforts should focus on initiatives that will open up productive opportunities for the poor.

- The MDBs need to go farther in developing mainstream alternatives to their standard product of large loans to a borrowing government, and install operating systems and staff incentives conducive to their success. These more flexible initiatives should build on the MDBs' ability to exert leadership, develop institutions, and make connections among disparate groups. They are staff- and relationship-intensive (with more diverse groups) and should be carefully tailored to the local situation. They include such things as removing legal or other roadblocks to the creation of microenterprises and of small firms seeking to utilize new publicly beneficial technologies in energy and other areas, and improving rural land markets. They may or may not be related to a sizable MDB loan. (See Recommendations 8a, 8b, and 8c beginning on page 57 and Recommendation 9 on page 69.)

❑ Environment: Making good on commitments

The MDBs should fully implement their existing environmental agendas and policies in such key areas as energy, forestry, resettlement, and pest management. Environmental and natural resource issues are public-policy concerns in which public institutions like the MDBs should play a leadership role. The MDBs have formulated a series of positive environmental initiatives, in areas such as energy conservation and assistance to environmentally sound enterprises, coupled with an extensive "do no harm" agenda, which should have served to avoid the kinds of harmful effects on the environment and local residents that have resulted from earlier MDB projects. These agendas have been implemented inconsistently. (See the discussion on page 31.)

MDB Operations

Recent studies as well as Task Force member experiences stirred concern that the MDBs need, as Task Force Cochair Senator Bill Bradley said, "to improve their performance as development actors."[1] The areas where the MDBs most need to improve—institutional development and achieving sustainable results (i.e., "the nonphysical construction" aspects of their mandate)—unfortunately are the areas in which the MDBs are likely to be needed most in the future and that cannot be devolved soon to the private sector.

These concerns led the Task Force to look at aspects of MDB operations and make recommendations for the following changes that appear to be essential corollaries to accomplishing the needed changes in MDB roles and functions:

❑ Flexibility

The MDBs should make more flexible the elements of their operating systems that combine to place institutional priority on large-scale lending. New processes and incentives need to be put in place that encourage staff to place priority on small projects, nonlending activities, and staff-intensive programs, when warranted by country circumstances. These more flexible processes and incentives need to be available across the full range of an institution's operations, not just to selected special programs. This increased flexibility should be extended where warranted to other areas such as procurement rules and project timetables that interfere with achievement of program objectives. (See Recommendation 9 on page 69.)

❑ Accountability

The persisting confusion over accountability for project implementation needs to be clarified. The MDBs should be accountable to their shareholders for following borrowers' implementation of projects closely enough to know if significant problems have developed, for getting the project back on track, and, if

---

1. Senator Bill Bradley, remarks at a CSIS Task Force meeting, Washington, D.C., September 26, 1996.

problems are not resolved, for canceling the loan and not making others to the same borrower. (See Recommendation 10 on page 70.)

❏ Links to local areas and people

An increasing share of MDB lending is intended to improve the lives of poor and vulnerable people. Yet much evidence has been brought forward of MDB programs that harmed or did not respond to the needs of poor people. It is important for the MDBs to develop better linkages to local groups and individuals through which they can determine the needs, views, and wishes of project beneficiaries and check on project implementation on the ground. In particular, they need to do the following:

• The MDBs need to develop means by which they ascertain the views of local people and take them into account throughout a project. (See Recommendation 11a on page 76.)

• The banks need to develop better means to know what is going on during project implementation and thereby improve their qualitative performance on the ground. As a first step, the banks should publish a report each year that reviews the status of all projects being implemented. This report would both show how well the banks are following project implementation and elicit useful information for the banks from outside sources. (See Recommendation 11b on page 79.)

❏ Internal incentives

The MDBs should comprehensively review their internal incentive structures and means of judging the performance of operational staff to reward progress toward economic, social, and environmental objectives, not the processing of large loans. (See Recommendation 13 on page 83.)

❏ Transparency

A persistent problem has been the enduring gap between MDB policies and public rhetoric on the one hand and what both systematic studies and anecdotal evidence show to be their performance on the other. This gap has been tolerated, in some cases by several generations of MDB managements. The group recommends that this discrepancy between policy and practice be closed, but in addition believes that this problem gives urgency to its recommendations to change the continuing MDB practice of keeping most of their operational documents confidential.

The group believes that the only way shareholders can know with confidence that the MDBs have changed their focus and are doing what is currently needed in a way that is likely to be successful is to open up their operations to more public scrutiny. Although the banks, of course, need to be able to hold members' national security information and proprietary business data confidential, their basic operating documents (such as their budgets, final-stage institutional planning documents, country lending strategies, and material on the status of upcoming and ongoing projects) should be available to the public upon request.

Additionally, as publicly funded institutions, the banks need to accept as legitimate the interest of citizens of all their members in key decisions that will affect the MDBs' future directions and performance, seeking to keep them informed of upcoming major policy choices about which interest has been demonstrated. The MDBs play a big role in matters that affect people's lives and depend on public confidence for their funding and leadership legitimacy. They must be prepared to demonstrate to taxpayers, as well as government leaders, that this confidence is warranted. (See Recommendation 12 on page 81 and Recommendation 14 on page 87.)

Checking on Bank Results

In the post–Cold War world where it is not considered enough just to transfer funds to friendly regimes, the banks must justify their funding by the quality of their programs. This means that the MDBs need evaluation systems that produce high-quality, independent judgments on whether bank programs achieved their objectives. To be credible to outside audiences, this evaluative material should be verifiable (i.e., with countries and projects identified), comprehensive, timely, and reasonably user friendly. It should be available to the public. If some or all of the MDBs cannot produce such material in one to two years, interested MDB members should consider forming an independent MDB evaluation group to evaluate the programs of those institutions. (See Recommendation 15 on page 91.)

Because one of the major weaknesses of MDB programs appears to be their sustainability, the banks should begin to check systematically on this and report periodically (perhaps every five years) on the status of projects that have been completed in the preceding period. In this way, taxpayers in donor and borrowing countries will know if their funds are producing continuing benefits. (See Recommendation 16 on page 92.)

Looking into the Future: Relevance and Priority Dependent on Performance

In looking at U.S. interests in the multilateral development banks, the Task Force clearly thought that their objectives remain vital for the United States, but each institution's ability to adapt to new challenges and produce high-quality results in more complex circumstances will determine its relevance and future priority.

Summary of Recommendations and Benchmarks

Access to Resources

1. Higher Threshold Standards for Country Policies.

   The MDBs should lend only to countries that are maintaining good economic, poverty reduction, and environmental policies.

   Each MDB has adopted policies and transparent procedures to do this.

2. Governance Adequate for Program Success.

   The MDBs should more actively support improved governance as a means to achieve economic growth and poverty reduction, and lend only to countries whose quality of governance is adequate for the success of MDB programs and the achievement of those objectives.

   Each MDB has adopted policies and procedures to look explicitly at the governance environment in each of its borrowers to determine whether it is adequate for the success of its programs.

3. Graduation.

   The MDBs should have clear graduation criteria from each of their facilities, transparent procedures (which are enforced) for applying them, and regular reviews of their adequacy.

   Each MDB has conducted a review of its graduation policies and means of applying them. The results are clear criteria and procedures that are being enforced.

Use of Resources

4. Fast-Disbursing Lending for Policy Reform.

   The MDBs should be much more selective concerning fast-disbursing, policy-based lending, lending only when reforms are strongly supported by the borrowing government, loan disbursement is closely linked to reform implementation, and the impact of reforms on all groups has been analyzed.

   Each MDB has adopted revised guidelines along these lines, and the loans they approve reflect them.

5. Avoiding Displacement of Private Funds.

   The MDBs should have much clearer and more systematic policies and procedures to assure that they do not displace available private funding or fund projects for which private funding would be available if the borrowing government adopted needed policy reforms.

   Each MDB has put in place such policies and procedures.

6. Financial Support for Private Projects.

    a.   Any private projects chosen for direct support should be selected by the MDBs through their country strategy process on the basis of contribution to development objectives. The MDBs need to have clear means by which they apply their normal project standards to private-sector projects they support.

        Each MDB has such processes and procedures and is enforcing them.

    b.   Four options are provided on the extent to which the MDBs should directly support private projects.

        See Recommendation 6b on page 49.

    c.   A decision should be made about whether to locate the World Bank Group's major center for responsibility for private transactions in the International Finance Corporation or in the Bank itself (with an appropriate change in the Bank's charter).

        A decision has been made on this matter and is being implemented.

7. Building on Country Commitment to Poverty Reduction.

The MDBs (except the EBRD) should adopt policies making a serious demonstrated commitment to poverty reduction a requirement for a lending program.

Each MDB has put in place such a policy and procedures to apply it.

8. Increasing the Productive Capacity of the Poor.

Direct MDB poverty reduction efforts should focus on initiatives that will open up productive opportunities for the poor, such as

    a.   Leadership to support small enterprise and microenterprise through strengthened policy dialogue, fostering linkages to commercial financial institutions, and coordinating capacity building for intermediary institutions;

    b.   Innovative approaches to helping small farmers take advantage of expanded market opportunities;

    c.   High-priority investments in human capital, when the MDBs' financial product and management capabilities are suited to project requirements.

Each MDB has reviewed its policies and lending portfolio and developed realistic plans that are consistent with its capabilities.

MDB Operations

9. Flexibility and Scale.

The MDBs should change and make more flexible the elements of their core processes and operating modalities, placing more emphasis on small scale programs where warranted.

Each MDB has adopted both core processes and staff incentives that encourage and facilitate priority attention, when warranted, to small projects, nonlending activities, and staff and leadership-intensive activities.

10. Accountability.

The MDBs should be considered accountable to their shareholders for the results of their projects, including for overseeing project implementation carefully enough to know if major problems threaten success and, if these problems cannot be solved, for stopping disbursement on the loan.

Each MDB has accepted this responsibility.

11. Links to Local Areas and People.

   a. The MDBs should develop specific modalities by which they assure an appropriate degree of participation by project beneficiaries in project development and implementation, including a screening process, a project cycle that accommodates participation, and a monitoring system to be sure that it happens.

   Each MDB has such a system in operation.

   b. The MDBs need to develop better means of checking on project implementation and assuring that changes are made when program objectives are threatened.

   Each MDB is producing status reports every year that give the status of each project being implemented, note where there are serious problems, and state who is responsible for remedial actions. These reports are made public.

12. Fixing the Gap between Rhetoric and Reality.

Each MDB should take effective steps to ensure that all parts of the institution follow established policies and that major discrepancies between institutional pronouncements and operational practice are curtailed.

Absence of instances where an MDB's operations contravene its policies or its practice diverges substantially from its public pronouncements. In cases where this has been a serious problem (e.g., various environmental policies in the World Bank), the problem has been resolved.

13. Incentives.

Each MDB should review comprehensively its incentive systems to ensure that they are signaling priority on success toward poverty reduction, economic growth, and environmental stewardship. Each MDB should devise a system by which organizational units and managements are rated by the results of their projects and the quality of their judgments toward achieving substantive objectives.

Each MDB has conducted such a review and made such changes.

14. Transparency.

The MDBs should change their policies on the public availability of documents to make many more documents public information (especially their basic operating documents), and in the case of particularly important documents to make them publicly available before final decisions on them are made. The MDBs should acknowledge as legitimate the interests of citizens of all shareholders in their key decisions, seeking to keep them informed of upcoming major policy choices about which interest has been shown.

Each MDB has changed its public information policies and practices along these lines. The World Bank is consulting with concerned groups as it "reformats its operational directives," and where there are divergent views on what aspects of policy documents should be mandatory requirements, these are referred to the Executive Board.

Evaluating Performance of the MDBs

15. Determining Results.

The MDBs should have evaluation systems that produce high-quality, independent judgments on whether bank programs achieved their objectives. This material should be verifiable, comprehensive, timely, reasonably user-friendly, and available to the public.

Each MDB has in place a system that meets these criteria and whose product inspires confidence in the quality and independent judgment of the system.

16. Tracking Sustainability.

To facilitate tracking the sustainability of MDB projects, the banks should report at least every five years on the status of their projects on which disbursements ended within the preceding five years. These reports should be verifiable and made available to the public.

Each MDB has initiated a system under which they compile such reports.

U.S. Financial Support

17. Approach to Determining U.S. Financial Participation.

The United States should base its financial contribution on the extent of mutual agreement with other bank shareholders on objectives and on bank performance in these areas, based on bank-by-bank scrutiny.

Not Applicable.

18. Timing of Reform.

Two variations are discussed on how rapidly progress toward suggested reforms should be expected and factored into decisions on U.S. funding.

Not Applicable.

CHAPTER 1

Introduction

A Changed World

The arena in which the multilateral development banks (MDBs) operate has changed almost beyond recognition since most of them were founded, and even since the last public assessment of U.S. participation in them was concluded in 1982.

End of the Cold War

The end of the Cold War has fundamentally transformed the world landscape and balance of power in ways that have important consequences for the MDBs. No longer is the ideological rivalry between the Soviet Union and the United States the central feature of the international system. As a result, the Western consensus on bolstering particular allies for security and political reasons, regardless of economic policy performance, has broken down. Meanwhile, economic and trade considerations have increased in importance.

Explosion of Debt and Budgetary Constraints

This period has also witnessed an explosion of debt both in the developed and developing world. For the donor countries, their budget constraints (and changing priorities due to the end of the Cold War) have resulted in greater scrutiny being applied to all spending, particularly that available for foreign aid. Many domestic constituencies and government officials in donor countries have seriously questioned the effectiveness of international aid, including their country's support for international lending. At a minimum, a number of U.S. decisionmakers are setting higher performance standards for international aid.

In parts of the developing world, debt is also increasing significantly and constraining those countries' budgetary choices.

Growth of World Output, Population, and Absolute Poverty

As global economic output increased fivefold from 1950 to 1990, world population doubled, and so did the number of people living in absolute poverty.

Changed Perceptions of the Role of Markets and the State

With the end of the Cold War, there is greater awareness concerning the importance of markets, but the application is far from uniform across all countries. National economic strategies throughout the world have shifted toward more market-oriented, open-trade approaches. It largely is agreed that although governments should set and enforce fair rules, the private sector should produce and sell goods at competitive market-determined prices. Increasingly, functions that used to be discharged by public or private monopolies, such as power generation and telephone service, are also being deemed to be provided more efficiently by competitive private producers, as long as an adequate regulatory framework exists. To finance this expansion of private activity, developing countries are striving to expand domestic capital markets.

More Sophisticated and Integrated International Capital Markets

There now is far more knowledge about developing-country borrowers, with a host of capital-market analysts around the world looking at almost all sovereign borrowers, many developing-country regional and state governments, and prominent local private firms. In addition, expectations of superior future returns in emerging markets have spawned the development of a variety of specialized instruments to meet the needs of developing-country projects, manage diverse risks, and potentially enable more specialized sources of capital (e.g., Western pension funds and insurance companies) to invest in developing markets. Such changes have enabled net private flows to developing countries to expand more than fivefold between 1990 and 1996 to $243.8 billion (while net MDB flows remained stable at about $15 billion).

But net private-sector flows are neither stable nor universal. Three-quarters of all private flows to developing countries are concentrated in 12 mostly large countries (accounting for 63 percent of the population of World Bank borrower countries), attracted by a variety of factors including resource endowments and country policies. In contrast, the poorest 60 "IDA-only" countries (accounting for 16 percent of total world population) receive only 1 percent of net private flows.

Emergence of Environmental Issues and Institutions

Among the most profound changes influencing the MDBs is the growing concern on the part of both governments and their citizens about environmental destruction and the rapidly escalating rates of use of natural resources. Many parts of the world have experienced degradation of forests, agricultural soils, and water supplies, which destroys productive assets and threatens human health and food supplies. Likewise, global warming, biodiversity loss, and ozone-layer depletion have alarmed many. Developing countries, where demand for energy, among other things, is skyrocketing, face especially important and difficult choices.

In addition to marking the transition to a new sustainable development paradigm, the 1992 United Nations Conference on Environment and Development spawned a host of institutions and commitments that provide a new reference point for MDB policies and lending.

Expansion of Other Nongovernmental Development Entities

There also has been a major expansion in many developing countries of private nonprofit entities working to foster various development and poverty reduction objectives. Some of these groups have grown enormously in scale of operation, sophistication, and the skill with which they accomplish their objectives. With increased activity, however, there are also increased chances that the nongovernmental organizations (NGOs) and the multilateral banks may duplicate each other's efforts or work at cross-purposes.

Likewise, much of the technical advisory services previously supplied by MDBs and other aid providers to developing countries are now readily available in all parts of the world from local or international private consultants.

The Information Age and Enhanced Communications Capabilities

Dramatic advances in information, communications, and transportation technology are strengthening the linkages between the most remote developing countries and the rest of the world, and offer the possibility of instant access even to remote rural villages. Students from Tashkent to Tanzania can log on to the Internet and access the most advanced information in many fields, and communicate with each other as well. Wireless telephone technology can bring advanced education, health services, and market data to isolated families and entrepreneurs. Although offering enormous potential, such technology will not be inexpensive, and differences between countries could be exacerbated unless policy conditions are created that will attract private investment and permit the spread of technological advances to the developing world.

Globalization of Trade and Investment

Increased integration has resulted from decreases in transportation and communication costs and barriers to trade, a convergence of customer preferences, changes in product and process technology, and an increased ability of firms to add value in different places (e.g., the paperwork of a U.S. health insurance firm is processed in a provincial city in India). These changes have provided new opportunities but also new challenges for developing countries. Many are attempting to modernize their institutions and economic structures to compete in this integrated global economy.

Maturing Governance: Growth in Adherence to the Objective of Accountable Democratic Government

Most developing countries at least publicly adhere to the rhetoric of an accountable government responsible to its citizens, although for many the practice is in fact quite different. As well, compared with 53 years ago, many more countries have made concrete moves toward adopting integral parts of the democratic model. Also, it has now been a generation since most developing countries that were ruled by colonial powers gained independence. In general, the ruling cadres in government and the private sector of these and other developing countries are much better educated and have the capacity to take advantage of their own and other countries' experiences and to be fully accountable for their own decisions.

Taking Account of Previous Experience

It has been 53 years since the Bretton Woods Conference created the World Bank, 50 years since President Truman started the first U.S. long-term development assistance program, and 35 years since President Kennedy reinvigorated U.S. development assistance with the Alliance for Progress. The regional MDBs, except the EBRD, have all been in operation for over 30 years. Although the information on that experience is not as accessible and has not been analyzed as thoroughly as it might be, we now have the opportunity to benefit from this extensive experience of both U.S. bilateral and multilateral foreign aid as we look at U.S. interests in and policy toward the MDBs.

Multilateral Development Banks: The Basics

The United States belongs to five MDBs: the World Bank Group, the African Development Bank (AfDB), the Asian Development Bank (ADB), the Inter-American Development Bank (IDB), and the European Bank for Reconstruction and Development (EBRD). It also belongs to the North American Development Bank (NAD Bank), a joint U.S.-Mexican institution intended to finance environmental infrastructure projects in both countries in order to facilitate implementation of the North American Free Trade Agreement, but because the objectives of this institution are so specialized, it is not covered as part of this project.

The MDBs are autonomous international agencies that finance economic and social development programs in developing countries using money borrowed in world capital markets or contributed by governments of the richer countries. Run by their own managements and staffs of international civil servants, they operate under the policy and operational direction of boards of executive directors and boards of governors selected by the member country governments. Countries' voting shares are based on their contributions to help finance MDB operations.

Although they differ substantially in the types of activities they fund, the MDBs' own sources and mechanisms for raising money are quite similar. Most of the MDBs have both a hard-term and a concessional-term lending window, and several MDBs (the World Bank, the IDB, and the AfDB) also have specialized affiliates for financing private-sector projects. They lend 75 percent of their funds on market terms, using money borrowed at commercial rates in world capital markets. These borrowings are backed by the capital subscriptions of their member countries. Part of this is paid-in capital. The rest is subject to call only if the MDBs need funds as a last resort to pay their creditors. The MDBs lend the other 25 percent of their funds on highly concessional terms, mainly to the poorest countries, using money contributed by their member country governments or repayments from previous loans.

The MDBs finance a wide range of types of projects. They generally finance about one-third of the costs of the projects they help support, the rest being financed by the borrower countries or by other lenders (e.g., commercial banks, export finance agencies, or other multilateral or bilateral aid agencies). Goods and services purchased as a result of MDB loans are subject to open international competitive bidding.

The World Bank Group

The World Bank Group, headquartered in Washington, D.C., is composed of the International Bank for Reconstruction and Development (IBRD), the International Development Association (IDA), the International Finance Corporation (IFC), the Multilateral Investment Guarantee Agency (MIGA), and the Global Environment Facility (GEF). By long-standing informal agreement, the president of the bank, currently James D. Wolfensohn, is a U.S. national.

The IBRD was created at Bretton Woods in 1944 by victorious countries of World War II who sought to develop a constructive framework for international finance in the postwar world. After the U.S. Marshall Plan was established in 1947 to finance postwar reconstruction, the IBRD's focus became development. Proposed by the United States, IFC was established as a private-sector funding affiliate in 1956 in response to pressure from developing countries to create a new UN fund as an alternative channel for foreign aid. IFC did not meet their expectations, however, and pressure resumed for a UN facility. Consequently, in 1960, the Eisenhower administration helped create IDA to provide concessional funding to poorer countries. MIGA was created in 1988 to fill a perceived gap in an investment insurance market unwilling to provide political-risk insurance to the extent required by private investors. GEF was established in 1990 by the World Bank Group and the United Nations as a three-year pilot program to provide supplementary financing to cover environmental costs relating to four global environmental issues: climate change, biological diversity, international waters, and depletion of the ozone layer. In 1994, a restructured GEF was established by participating governments as an independent organization. The World Bank's role in the restructured GEF is as a trustee of the GEF trust fund and as an implementing agency along with the United Nations.

The Regional Development Banks

Asian Development Bank. The Asian Development Bank (ADB) was created in 1966 to fulfill the multiple purposes of advancing economic and social development in the region, funding the rehabilitation of Indochina, and strengthening U.S. ties across the Pacific. It is headquartered in Manila, Philippines. The president of the Bank, by custom a Japanese national, is currently Mitsuo Sato.

Loans from the hard window totaled $4.05 billion in 1995. The ADB's concessional facility, the Asian Development Fund, set up in 1974, committed $1.45 billion to the poorest developing member countries in 1995.

African Development Bank. The African Development Bank (AfDB), established in 1964, aims to further the socioeconomic development of African countries, individually and collectively. To this end, the Bank promotes the investment of private and public capital for development, primarily by providing loans for projects and programs that contribute to the growth and development of African economies.

The limited ability of many African countries to borrow AfDB resources on nonconcessional terms led, in 1972, to the establishment of the African Development Fund (AfDF) with resources mobilized from donor contributions. In 1982, with the goal of strengthening the Bank's standing in world capital markets, nonregional countries were allowed to purchase a nonmajority interest in the AfDB. The United States became a member in 1983.

In 1996, the most recent lending year, AfDB loans amounted to $500 million while AfDF loans came to $300 million.

Inter-American Development Bank. In 1959, the first of the regional development banks, the Inter-American Development Bank (IDB) was established as a response to the desire of countries in the Western Hemisphere for an international financial institution that would be more regionally sensitive and would improve U.S. relations with the region. Though the IDB has welcomed nonregional members since 1970, Latin American countries still have been able to retain their small majority of voting power (50.02 percent). Currently Enrique Iglesias of Uruguay serves as president.

In 1996, the Bank approved a total of $6.7 billion in loans. The regular lending window provides most of the IDB's resources; $6.375 billion was committed in 1996. The Fund for Special Operations (FSO), the Bank's soft window, lends to the poorest countries. In 1996, the FSO approved 22 new loans totaling $394 million. A small third window, the Intermediate Finance Facility (IFF), lends at terms intermediate to the hard and soft window by using the Bank's net income to subsidize the cost of borrowing countries' regular loans. In 1996, $267 million was channeled through this account.

In 1984 the IDB created a small affiliate, the Inter-American Investment Corporation (IIC), which makes loans without government repayment guarantees to stimulate growth of private-sector firms. In 1996, IIC authorized 20 transactions totaling $72 million. Another small affiliate, the Enterprise for the Americas Multilateral Investment Fund (MIF) provides grant financing for activities designed to expand marginal groups' participation in the economy and finance microenterprises in Latin America. In 1996, MIF financed 46 projects totaling $76.2 million.

European Bank for Reconstruction and Development. The European Bank for Reconstruction and Development (EBRD) was created in April 1991 to help countries of central and eastern Europe make the transition toward market-oriented economies. Located in London, the Bank's mandate is unique in that it includes a political element: recipient governments must be committed to applying the principles of multiparty democracy, pluralism, and market economics. With no concessional window, the EBRD lends only at market rates. As set out in its charter, 60 percent of funds must be lent to or invested in private-sector or privatizing public-sector firms, and it may lend without government guarantees. The president of the Bank is Jacques de Larosière from France.

CHAPTER 2

Conclusions

U.S. Interests in the MDBs

Objectives Are in U.S. Interest

The MDBs' objectives of reducing poverty, stimulating broad-based economic growth, and promoting environmental sustainability in developing countries continue to be important U.S. interests. They are key prerequisites to reducing political and social instability abroad, which, if left unchecked, has enormous security, economic, and social costs for the United States and the developing world. The United States has a very large stake in the environmental choices made by developing countries, and pervasive poverty often results in migration, drug production, and crime.

If achieved, the MDBs' objectives will provide a powerful stimulus for international economic growth and provide significant trade and commercial opportunities for the United States. Currently 50 percent of U.S. agricultural commodities go to the poorer countries of the world, as do 40 percent of our total goods and services. If the poor in developing countries can move productively into the economic mainstream, they will not only stimulate economic development in their own countries but will accelerate global growth and expand the market for U.S. products.

Advantages for Achieving Objectives

As instruments for achieving these objectives, the MDBs have significant advantages:

❏ Flexible and relatively cost-effective means of raising funds because of their ability to share funding requirements broadly among countries and tap capital markets cheaply (i.e., U.S. funding leverages substantial funding from others).

❏ Significant existing financial capital and intellectual talent drawn from all parts of the world.

❏ Established role as a clearinghouse for much valuable information.

❏ Accepted leadership role in the international economic system and accustomed source of advice for borrowers. Such advice may be less likely to elicit a nationalistic response than if given by the United States alone. This is made possible by the MDBs' multinational character and historic role.

In addition, even though the United States at times may have used its influence unwisely, or failed to use it in some areas, the United States still has the potential to exercise leadership disproportionate to its funding in the MDBs due to its historical role and associated privileges (e.g., naming the president of the World Bank).

Obstacles to Achieving Objectives

The MDBs also have disadvantages, however, many of which were caused by their shareholders (including the United States):[2]

☐ They have accumulated disparate and sometimes contradictory roles and functions. Too often they have not eliminated outdated functions or established clear priorities among functions. Sometimes they have taken on new functions but not made the concomitant changes required to perform the functions well. This may stem from the different views of their various shareholders and the lack of mechanisms to force resolution of differences.

☐ In some areas, they have outdated and inflexible structures and requirements that limit effectiveness.

☐ Most have become large, change-resistant, opaque bureaucracies. This makes it hard to tell what initiatives are serious priorities and which are public-relations trappings. For some, policy decisions are not well integrated into the project identification and design process.

☐ Most have evolved incentive structures that emphasize quantity of lending over quality and over important nonlending activities.

U.S. Policy

In light of the significant changes that have taken place, the MDBs face the need to make major changes and reforms in their operations. The United States should have a clear vision of the role it wants the MDBs to play and support a well-defined set of policy changes and structural reforms within the institutions to support that vision.

The key to the MDBs' usefulness to the United States will be whether they can terminate outdated functions and ways of doing business, even when these were highly congenial to some of their borrowers and their managers, and move on to functions and operating modalities that are priorities now. In many cases, these changes will be difficult and require a focus on different activities, operating strengths, and staff skills. Institutions like the MDBs and the pursuit of their objectives are very much still needed. The question is whether these institutions can make the changes and reforms required to fulfill their objectives in today's environment.

As the United States seeks to implement its policy vision for the MDBs, U.S. policy for the various institutions should be translated into monitorable steps so

---

2.   Many of these do not apply to the much newer EBRD.

that all U.S. stakeholders can follow progress. Progress toward U.S. objectives must be clear because hard budget choices will need to be made.

U.S. Financial Support

Spending for the MDBs should provide results and benefits that, although indirect for U.S. citizens, are at least equivalent to those from other types of government spending. If the MDBs can make substantial progress toward their objectives, they are priority uses of U.S. resources. Their ability to do this, however, varies by bank and depends on their ability to focus clearly on currently needed functions and to improve effectiveness. They also need much more systematic, rigorous, and transparent vehicles for shareholders to evaluate the results of their work.

A sizable majority of the Task Force rejected making a decision that no new funding would be needed for the MDBs or a decision that they should continue to receive the same level of real resources. Most members thought that the United States should look at each institution and base future U.S. funding on how well it has adapted to new priorities and the quality of its programs in pursuit of them.

Role of the MDBs

In Need of Reexamination and Change

Since their inception, the MDBs have taken on a number of roles—as bankers, as aid agencies, as consulting firms, and as purveyors of leverage to induce policy reforms. Recent global political and economic changes have affected all of these roles.

❏ The MDBs' financial intermediation or banking function, channeling funds to potentially financially viable projects, is now needed in fewer countries, sectors, and projects in light of the development of private capital markets. Some of the private funding is very volatile, however, and can flow out swiftly, at times in response to factors that are not subject to country influence. In these situations MDB flows can play a stabilizing role. The MDBs must substantially upgrade their ability and willingness to target their resource transfers to where they are still needed and where conditions prevail that will permit achievement of program objectives.

❏ The MDBs' aid function—channeling resources to projects that have potentially high social, economic, and environmental returns but cannot attract private funding—has come under increased pressure to demonstrate effectiveness as support for Cold War–motivated transfers declines and as examples of unsuccessful programs receive more attention. Of particular concern is whether the standard MDB product—large loans made by headquarters-based staff who rely on the borrowing government to check on implementation and monitor who gets the benefits—can be relied on to achieve objectives in projects that seek to safeguard the environment or reduce poverty.

❑ The MDBs' consulting-firm or technical-advice function, although highly regarded and sought in many cases, faces competition from private firms and other purveyors of these services (e.g., universities and research institutes in developing and developed countries). At the same time, experience is revealing the importance of specific local knowledge (which is often not an MDB strength) in a wider variety of disciplines.

❑ The MDBs' ability to exert leverage for policy changes has waned in some countries as private financial flows assume greater importance; in other countries, experience has revealed the complex requirements for success in this area. If policy prescriptions are not based on in-depth local knowledge and do not result from a broad-based local process and choices, they are unlikely to be consistently and successfully implemented.

Although the limits of the MDBs' direct leverage in changing borrower policies may be greater and better understood than in the past, the role these institutions can play in analyzing and providing suggestions about country policies remains important. Private financiers usually are less well suited to looking comprehensively at country economic policies, particularly at political and social factors. Therefore, they often value and carefully consider the MDBs' analyses and judgments.

❑ The MDBs' ability to convene or bring together diverse groups both within countries and among countries may have been underestimated and perhaps underutilized. The MDBs have a unique range of contacts within developing countries and are thus well placed to exert leadership to get parties with different interests and perspectives to work together in a harmonious and unthreatening environment. Likewise, the MDBs continue to provide a useful framework through which different countries can address common problems together.

As the MDBs try to react to these changes, they are hindered by the divergent opinions of other shareholders, some of which may be amenable to change if the United States makes a convincing case for its priorities, and by entrenched interests both within and outside the banks that benefit from existing MDB programs and policies.

The Task Force devoted most of its time to looking at how the role of the MDBs should change. It first looked at several areas where the MDBs should more precisely target their efforts. Then the group looked at the areas where it believed that changes in MDB functions were needed. These included the amount and type of fast-disbursing lending to support policy changes, how the relationship between the MDBs and private funds should change with the huge expansion in private flows to some of the MDBs' biggest borrowers, and the role the MDBs should play in poverty reduction. The group thought the MDBs' role should be:

❐ *Limited in Duration and More Sharply Focused*

The MDBs should see their financial role as a transitional one in which their success is measured by the countries and sectors in which their lending activities become unnecessary because their objectives have been accomplished or because the country now can meet its financial needs with domestic and commercial sources of capital. As more members graduate from receiving loans, the institutions should consider, as the ADB is now, whether and how they best can use their expertise and channels for collaboration for the benefit of their members in nonlending activities. Those institutions, such as the IDB and the ADB, that have long served as important consultative forums on regional problems should certainly continue and perhaps expand this role even as the need for new lending to some members declines.

In general, the MDBs should examine in detail the many changes that have taken place and eliminate those functions that either are no longer high priorities or are not suited to the products, in terms of resource packages, expertise, or influence, that they can bring to bear.

❐ *Limited to Borrowers Making a Significant Effort to Help Their Own People*

One of the strongest and most well-documented lessons of the last 30 years is that providing external resources in the absence of adequate borrower economic, social, and environmental policies is ineffective and sometimes counterproductive. The MDB practice of selectively cutting off lending to a few egregious nonperformers, while allowing others to continue to borrow, has been neither fair nor effective.

The MDBs should establish a significantly higher, more transparent, and more consistent threshold of adequacy for borrower policies that must be crossed before borrowers receive more than nominal resources. This threshold should include not just economic policies but also policies directed at reducing poverty and ensuring responsible environmental stewardship.

The MDBs' active borrowers should be limited to countries whose overall policy environment is deemed in transparent and comprehensive analysis to be sufficiently adequate to lead to broad-based sufficiently sustainable economic growth. A particular area of analysis should be how the country mobilizes and uses its own resources, because MDB funds received by governments are clearly fungible into general budget expenditures. Because a major U.S. interest in the MDBs is reducing poverty, a significant part of a determination of policy adequacy must include policies that make it possible for the poor to participate fully in and benefit from growth (e.g., taxation and regulatory policies, use of domestic resources).

Citizens of countries failing to meet these criteria should be assisted through the programs of other donors aimed at direct humanitarian relief (i.e., various UN agencies, bilateral donors, NGOs).

❏ *Limited to Borrowers Where Governance Is Adequate to Permit Program Success*

The Task Force encountered much evidence that failures in the quality of borrowing-country governance often have been major causes of failures of MDB programs. Therefore, to improve results, the MDBs should be more active in the governance area in two ways:

- The MDBs should be more attuned to borrowing-country governance problems that could interfere with program success. Lending should be curtailed when such things as lack of accountability/corruption, lack of respect for property rights and the rule of law, or lack of concern for the welfare of the borrowing country's own citizens and their ability to have meaningful input into program formulation substantially undercut prospects for economic growth or program success. Meeting minimum standards in terms of quality of governance should become a key factor in receive new MDB funding.

- The MDBs should take a more proactive stance to assure that governance problems do not undercut the success of ongoing activities. This means making more aggressive efforts to investigate complaints about governance problems in projects, taking tougher stands (e.g., canceling projects) when problems go unremedied, and making more active and consistent efforts to assure that bank projects are taking account of the needs and views of local groups, rather than saying that this is a matter to be left to the preferences of the borrowing government.

In addition, the banks should work to make their own decisionmaking more transparent and their project selection and design process more open to input from diverse local groups so as to serve as a better model for borrowing-country governance.

Fast-Disbursing Lending to Support Policy Changes

Although the Task Force concluded that adequate borrower policies are a necessity for successful development, the group believed that MDB programs to provide fast-disbursing loans conditioned on future policy change have had a problematic track record and have been used in too many situations where the preconditions for success were not in place. The perceived need by both MDBs and borrowing governments for quick resource transfers has often led to agreement on policy reforms that were not fully supported by borrowing governments or endorsed by broader civil society elements, frequently resulting in incomplete implementation. On occasion this has reduced the urgency for reforms. The MDBs should be much more selective about the conditions under which they deploy this type of loan.

Infrastructure: Still a Priority, But More Selectivity Needed

The Task Force thought that infrastructure development remains very important for economic growth, poverty reduction, and environmental sustainability. Some types of infrastructure construction (such as potable water and sewage) have been particularly successful for the MDBs. The group had two major concerns about the MDBs' role:

❑ How quickly is it possible and desirable for private funds to take over the financing of various types of infrastructure? The MDBs must hit a fine line between (1) preempting private-sector solutions or pressure for borrower policy improvements to make these available and (2) too-rapid pullouts where private options are not available but there is evidence that traditional infrastructure projects can be successful and sustainable.

❑ Problems of operating entities. Some types of infrastructure (such as construction of large dams) have proven problematic for the MDBs and others have had major sustainability problems (usually resulting from poor performance of operating institutions). In some cases, numerous MDB attempts at technical assistance or conditions attached to loans have failed to solve problems, which stem from political rather than technical capacity problems. The MDBs should be more realistic in assessing risks and not lend until there is compelling evidence that the root causes of institutional failure have been resolved.

The MDBs and the Private Sector: A Means to Broad-Based Growth and Poverty Reduction

The MDBs should play a leadership role in helping their borrowers move into and adapt to the increasingly integrated and competitive global economy. Only by maximizing their comparative advantages in the international market system can developing countries share in accelerated economic growth and widening opportunities. This will require borrowing countries to create conditions conducive to private-sector-led growth. The development of the private sector, both domestic and foreign, promotes market-based growth, which combined with the right complementary policies helps to alleviate poverty.

Rapid changes often bring perils for some, however, and the MDBs should be in the forefront as well in helping their borrowers analyze which groups will be hurt, at least temporarily, by changes and how hardship can be avoided or mitigated.

The Regulatory Framework and Institutions to Enforce It. Task Force members believe that the MDBs can play an important role in helping their borrowers to create and enforce the policy and regulatory framework needed both to attract private-sector development and to protect the interests of the public and its most vulnerable segments from corrupt distortions of it. The MDBs are especially suited to do this because of their recognized role as impartial international public institutions and their ability to bring to bear high-quality technical expertise and the lessons of international experience.

The MDBs should help their borrowers create both the rules and the institutional framework to enforce them for markets (including local financial markets) to function efficiently and fairly. They should help to devise a reliable framework for safeguarding property rights (including intellectual property), rights of association, and the rights of women and minorities to own property.

At the same time, the MDBs are well positioned to play a leadership role in pushing for a regulatory framework that fully and responsibly deals with public-policy issues, especially environmental and natural-resource management, competition policy, protecting the public safety, and preventing monopolies and crony capitalism.

The Task Force was divided in how effective it thought the MDBs were in performing this function. There was support for more active MDB leadership efforts in several areas, especially setting common standards for all private participants in public-policy areas and for more in-depth attention to the important, but less visible, areas of improved business practices such as corporate governance, access to arbitration, rules concerning mortgages and liens, foreign-exchange conversion, and accounting and financial disclosure. There was strong support for recent active MDB efforts, such as the EBRD's leadership in discouraging Russian companies from restricting shareholder voting rights and the ADB's tough message to Vietnam on improving public management.

However, considerable concern was expressed over the MDBs' poor track record in helping to strengthen the borrower institutions needed to enforce and adapt new regulatory frameworks fairly, once they have been put in place. The development of these institutions, from environmental enforcement agencies to rural land registries to stock-market regulatory entities, is critical to efficient and fair private-sector development and should be areas of important MDB impact but seem to be caught up in pervasive MDB problems in achieving institutional development objectives (see Recommendation section on MDB Operations).

Avoiding Displacement of the Private Sector. The MDBs must develop more systematic and transparent measures to ensure that they do not delay the development of local private sectors or international private flows by funding projects in the public sector in situations where, if the borrower followed appropriate policies, private funding would be available. This becomes ever more important as private capital becomes available for more types of projects in more countries.

Obviously, even in potentially commercially viable sectors there are cases where public funding may be needed to correct externalities or market failures. Cases where the borrowing country simply prefers to pursue public-sector options with MDB funding, however, do not provide a good reason for the MDB to proceed. It is not acceptable for U.S. taxpayers to subsidize nonmarket choices when private funding is available, unless transparent public-policy reasons for such an exception can be shown and alternatives appear likely to produce a better result.

Direct MDB Support for Private Projects. The issue on which Task Force members were most clearly divided was whether MDB efforts to fund directly projects containing private investment should be substantially increased.

This issue has assumed greater significance in recent years, given the pioneering efforts of some countries to allow the private sector to fund, build, and own new infrastructure projects. These projects previously were funded by the public sector, often with sizable MDB financing. These private projects often offer major improvements in construction and operating efficiency, and at times in environmental soundness. They also relieve strained budgets and conserve debt-servicing capacity.

Usually private financiers are willing to assume commercial risks, and sound projects in countries pursuing appropriate policies can attract sufficient equity and short-term debt finance. Long-term debt financing can be problematic, however, when investors are concerned about future government actions and political stability. The types of political risk involved may be either so hard to assess or of such magnitude that many commercial sources of finance are not willing or able to deal with them. MDB involvement is perceived by many private investors to mitigate this risk, by providing reassurance that the MDBs will intercede in case a future government tries to change the rules of the game.

Current MDB programs to fill gaps in funding for large infrastructure projects are small in relation to the size of the projects, hemmed in by many limitations and fragmented among MDB organizational entities.

Some Task Force members thought that the advantages of shifting important infrastructure to the private sector, the ability of small amounts of MDB funding or contingent liabilities to leverage much larger private financing, and the MDBs' comparative advantage as an interlocutor with borrowing governments argued strongly for a major enhancement in their programs of this type.

Others were concerned about resources for private projects "crowding out" projects for which private capital is not available and were concerned that the MDBs' staff skills and incentives do not equip them well for private programs. Above all, some Task Force members thought that the MDBs' lack of agility in terminating outdated programs could lead to the continuation of subsidies to private producers after any short-term justification had disappeared. Specific views of Task Force members are discussed in detail concerning Recommendation 6b.

The MDBs and Poverty Reduction

Reducing poverty in developing countries is important to the United States for political/security, economic, and humanitarian reasons. Therefore, officially supported lending institutions such as the MDBs should play a significant role in grappling with this major international problem. The Task Force agreed on the following:

❑ Broad-based economic growth is indispensable, but not in itself sufficient, for any strategy to reduce poverty.

❏ A particularly important role the MDBs can perform in reducing poverty is to establish clearly that demonstrated borrower commitment to poverty reduction and broadly sharing the benefits of growth is necessary for significant MDB lending.

❏ In their own poverty reduction activities, the MDBs should focus on strategies that give poor people the ability to participate fully in economic growth, especially programs that enable them to acquire and empower them to use productive assets. This would include

- the complex of activities that facilitate small business and micro-enterprise, especially policies and regulations that permit small business to enter and compete in markets freely;

- the range of investments from rural roads to strengthening of property rights and market-based producer support services that make trade and market-led development work for small-scale agricultural producers; and

- investments in human capital, where the needs of the project are well suited to the products the MDBs can offer, including loans that must be repaid in foreign exchange.

The MDBs and the Environment

A number of members of the Task Force began with the preconception, which turned out to be incorrect, that so much attention has been devoted to MDB problems concerning the environment and so much effort made for over a decade to secure approval of good MDB environmental policies, improved procedures (especially as mandated in the "Pelosi Amendment" passed by the U.S. Congress), and substantially enlarged MDB environmental staffs that these issues have been satisfactorily resolved. Instead, the Task Force encountered much evidence that many of the improved policies have not been translated into changes in how the MDBs were functioning, especially in how projects were being implemented on the ground. (Examples are noted in Appendix D.)

There was also concern that the banks are not taking sufficient account of the limitations posed in particular cases by finite resources, and there was support for the banks making efforts to develop the best tools possible to evaluate the stocks and flows of resources—environmental, human, and financial.

The set of problems found in implementing the improved environmental policies appear also to be impacting many other MDB activities that require changes in institutions, policies, and practices that are complex to implement and that challenge vested interests. These problems include lack of well-functioning linkages between the MDBs and the areas where their projects are implemented, lack of accountability (especially for project implementation), and persistent tolerance for wide discrepancies between MDB policies/public pronouncements and on-the-ground performance. These concerns led the Task Force to focus more than was planned on a set of MDB operational issues that appear to be the cause of the problems.

MDB Operations

Although some MDB projects are successful, numerous studies and Task Force member observations gave the Task Force cause for concern that the MDBs are having difficulty meeting their objectives in projects such as institutional development, financial reform, and macroeconomic and sector reform—that is, activities aimed at "nonphysical results" (as compared with constructing things). Likewise, the few studies available indicate doubts that over one-half of recently evaluated World Bank projects will be able to sustain their benefits after external funding has ceased.

These findings were the cause of particular concern because it is this kind of "nonphysical" project for which private funding is least likely to be available and for which MDB efforts are most important.

The Task Force then considered why these problems are continuing and concluded that although some changes have been made, they have not been sufficiently fundamental, far-reaching, and consistent as the relative priority for MDB efforts has shifted from large loans for constructing infrastructure in the public sector to a variety of complex tasks requiring different approaches and skills (e.g., developing regulatory institutions, reforming management systems, implementing natural-resource conservation activities, better targeting public services on those who need them). In some cases, the banks' public rhetoric and policies have changed, while their practices have not.

The Task Force considered what changes might produce improvements, and these included establishing clearer accountability for project implementation, greater flexibility in a variety of areas (including improving staff incentives to devote time to small projects), altering existing operating modalities to get better information about how projects are working in the field and to translate the rhetoric on beneficiary participation into reality, and trying to narrow the gap between MDB policies/public statements and their products (Recommendations 9–13).

Evaluating Performance of the MDBs

In view of the strong evidence that simply providing money to developing countries does not necessarily produce good economic, social, or political results, the MDBs should take very seriously their responsibility to demonstrate the quality of their performance and the benefits that have resulted from their expenditures.

Transparency

The Banks should become much more transparent, with most of their operating documents (other than proprietary business data or material concerning members' national security) available upon request. This would include major planning and budget documents, information on upcoming projects, and data on the status of ongoing projects.

In the case of specific projects, the end of the banks' secrecy about planning documents on future projects would not only respond to legitimate requests by those likely to be affected, but should also improve the quality of bank projects, because many have suffered from lack of sufficient knowledge about the local situation. Likewise, the proposal made in Recommendation 11, for the banks to report publicly on the status of ongoing projects, should help them to get accurate information about ongoing operations from a much broader perspective.

For issues that have a major bearing on future MDB strategic directions and the quality of their product, the MDBs should take a more forthcoming approach on public interest and views, both because the quality of their work has broad impact and because perceptions about their performance among concerned U.S. groups will have a bearing on their budget priority in the United States.

Results of Bank Projects

It is very important to have reliable means to evaluate the results of the various MDBs' work. These results are not available now, because the MDBs' evaluation systems are only geared to an internal audience, produce material of varying quality, and keep most of their evaluation material confidential.[3]

It will be critical for U.S. support for the institutions to have available comprehensive, verifiable, clear, timely, and public material produced by a credible evaluation entity. This material should relate funds expended to program achievements in a verifiable (i.e., country and project specific) and understandable way. (The World Bank's Operations Evaluation Department, which reports directly to its board rather than Bank management, produces such good-quality material, but it is often kept confidential and is designed for internal use. It is not clear whether the other MDBs, whose evaluation units do not have similar independent reporting arrangements, could produce material of comparable quality.)

If the MDBs cannot put in place within one to two years systems that give credible and understandable results (such as is described in Recommendation 15), shareholders should establish an independent body outside the MDBs to perform the evaluation function regarding those institutions that are not making available adequate material.

Sustainability: Tracking Completed Projects

In order to improve further shareholders' ability to judge the value of the MDBs' work and enhance an MDB focus on long-term sustainable results, the MDBs should track and regularly report on the operational status of projects upon which disbursements have been completed.

---

3.   The World Bank does make available many (although not all) of its evaluation products, including some quite sensitive material.

In looking at U.S. interests in the multilateral development banks, the Task Force clearly thought that their objectives remain vital for the United States, but each institution's ability to adapt to new challenges and produce high-quality results in more complicated circumstances will determine its relevance and future priority.

CHAPTER 3

Recommendations

The following are the specific recommendations of the Task Force for changes to be advocated by the United States in the MDBs and suggested benchmarks by which U.S. policymakers may know whether they are being adopted. As could be expected, all recommendations do not apply equally to all MDBs due to differences in borrowing-country circumstances, mandates of the various institutions, and institutional performance. Where the Task Force believes there are major differences in application of a recommendation, this is noted.

ACCESS TO MDB RESOURCES: Higher Threshold Standards of Country Policy Adequacy

Background

Over the last several years, most of the MDBs have adopted country borrowing eligibility and allocation criteria to link in some way funds lent to the borrowing country's economic policy performance. These linkages have generally been loosely or inconsistently applied, however, and have failed to stop the flow of MDB funds to countries whose policy frameworks are inadequate to support sustainable economic growth and poverty reduction.

Some of the weaknesses of current MDB systems include the following:

❑ Adequacy of the economic policy framework is often only one of several allocation criteria, which may also include total population, need, and access to other resources. Such systems easily can result in substantial resources being diverted to countries whose policy framework is not adequate to produce desired results.

❑ Some allocation systems implicitly "grade on the curve," so some countries' policies are deemed acceptable because they are marginally better than their neighbors', even if they are not adequate to produce sustainable growth and poverty reduction.

❑ Some MDBs will make large project loans if the immediate sector policies are adequate, even if the broad country policy framework is severely flawed. This often is done when the country's resources are used for massive subsidies to state-owned enterprises or for military hardware or are subject to leakage due to corruption. The scale of misuse of resources is often so large that it dwarfs any funding that outsiders could make available. For example, the World Bank estimates that for all countries in Africa (not all of which are MDB borrowers), the drain from public enterprises and losses in the financial system is 8–12 percent of GDP, which is two to three times greater than the amount spent on health and education and about two-thirds of gross investment.[4]

❐ In spite of MDBs' rhetoric that their major objective is poverty reduction, adequate country policies to permit their own poor to share in growth are seldom required for MDB lending. Likewise, MDBs seldom look at whether environmental policies are adequate to permit growth to be sustained.

❐ Most MDB country eligibility and lending allocation decisions are made in such untransparent ways that the factors that lead to decisions are nearly untraceable by outsiders.[5]

Change Needed

On the basis of numerous studies and much past experience, the Task Force believes that the MDBs should only conduct lending operations in countries that are maintaining a policy framework adequate to permit economically, environmentally, and socially sustainable growth. Countries that do not maintain policies adequate to support economic growth do not have the financial resources to invest in their people and are tempted to deplete natural resources. Countries that do not invest in their own people, including their poor, are wasting potentially valuable resources, often impel their neglected citizens to overconsume valuable natural resources, and undercut U.S. objectives in providing funding to developing countries. Economic growth will not be sustainable and will certainly not lead to poverty reduction if it is achieved by liquidating a country's natural resources base, destroying productive ecosystem functions, and contaminating air, water, and soils.

Criteria. Obviously, it is impossible to formulate universally applicable specific criteria for policy adequacy in each of these areas, but the following are the kinds of issues to be examined:

❐ Economic policies—substantial freedom from restriction on prices and production, adequate fiscal and monetary policies, policies needed for domestic and foreign investment, policies that safeguard property rights, and the limitation of the public sector to appropriate activities only.

❐ Policies toward the poor—where the tax burden falls, the regulatory framework affecting the poor (including barriers to labor use and the operation of

---

4. World Bank, "Private Sector Development in Low-Income Countries," *Development in Practice* (Washington, D.C.: World Bank, 1995), cited by John Mullen, "Private Sector Development and Poverty Reduction: Are they Linked?" (paper prepared for the CSIS Task Force on the United States and the MDBs, Washington, D.C., 1996), 5.

5. The African Development Bank has somewhat more specific and transparent criteria (especially for its concessional window), which are negotiated by its members in funding replenishment negotiations.

small businesses and microenterprises), and the allocation of government resources (both among and within sectors).

❏ Environmental stewardship—laws, regulatory structure, and enforcement practices that take account of concern for sustainable use of natural resources.

There may be trade-offs among these objectives, and there is no way this Task Force can prejudge specific future decisions, which will need to be made by MDB officials at the time in light of particular circumstances. (Some of these trade-offs will probably involve the value accorded to future benefits compared with current costs.) This recommendation is intended to eliminate lending to countries not because they make choices among legitimate objectives, but for pursuing policies that appear to support no legitimate objective or divert major resources to special interests. For example, this policy adequacy test would not be met by governments that are expending large amounts of their own resources on unneeded military purchases or money-losing state enterprises, or whose leaders are appropriating sizable sums for their own use.

Specific policies developed locally. For countries that have demonstrated convincing commitment to these policy objectives, greater emphasis should be placed by the MDBs on encouraging locally developed policy packages, local selection among options, and formulation of specific programs. Only in this way can borrowing governments assume responsibility for their country's future and move toward graduation from reliance on external support.

The MDBs should encourage thorough local discussion of policy options, which is likely to lead to more-implementable policies that better reflect local situations. At times, the process of policy selection itself will have a bearing on judgments about whether policy options are reasonable and fair choices under the circumstances.

In deciding upon whether a country's policies merit MDB lending, senior officials of the institutions will need to rely on their own best judgment about whether the policies can produce the desired result.

Application of higher standards of policy adequacy. The MDBs should develop and announce higher threshold criteria of policy adequacy. These criteria would apply to all windows of the institution. Other allocation criteria, such as population size or need, should only be applied to the universe of countries meeting the policy adequacy standard. The procedure for applying these standards should be as transparent as possible, and the resulting decisions should be considered public information.

Countries that do not meet policy adequacy standards. For countries not meeting these criteria, the MDBs should make every effort to maintain an active dialogue and continue policy, analytical, and sector work and technical assistance to try to help such countries identify and deal with policy problems. The MDBs should not provide financial resources, however, because this may serve to delay reform.

In certain clearly defined cases, it is in the international community's interest to provide funds for certain projects as much as it is in that of the country where the activity is taking place. These cases would include funding to contain health or safety hazards (such as epidemics) that could spread across borders, funding to reduce global environmental threats, and funding to stabilize postconflict situations. In these cases, it is unrealistic or counterproductive to impose the normal policy adequacy requirement. Such "global benefit" criteria should be carefully and sharply defined, however, and any MDB lending to be approved under this criterion should be clearly specified and not commingled with regular MDB lending. In many situations of this type, funding from bilateral donors or UN agencies may be more appropriate.

Lending to cover debt service. Although it is not possible to know how much MDB lending has been made for "defensive lending" purposes, it is likely that debt-service coverage concerns have skewed MDB lending in favor of poor performers and have influenced the banks to inflate the size of some loans beyond what project considerations would dictate. Although the advantages and disadvantages of particular multilateral debt "exit strategy" proposals were not considered by the Task Force, continuation of extensive "defensive lending" is one of the worst options. Continuation of this practice would virtually preclude adoption of the higher threshold standards that this Task Force believes to be critical.

The poor-country debt problem should be dealt with frankly and transparently. An initiative that attempts to address this problem was launched at the 1996 World Bank annual meeting, but it is not clear that negotiations on specific aspects will result in resolution of the problem.

It is also important that if an exit strategy proposal is implemented, the MDBs not begin again the practices that led to the buildup of this problem. In particular, lending should not occur to countries whose policies are not adequate to achieve objectives. Also, the lesson should be learned that for many countries, even concessional-term lending (which must be repaid in convertible currencies) can become a large burden and must be incurred only sparingly and for expenditures that require foreign exchange.

> **RECOMMENDATION 1. Access to MDB Resources: Higher Threshold Standards of Country Policy Adequacy.** The MDBs should lend only to countries that are maintaining a policy framework adequate to achieve economically, environmentally, and socially sustainable growth. This means demonstrated commitment to poverty reduction, environmental stewardship, and sound economic policies.

> ***BENCHMARK.*** *Each MDB has adopted country lending allocation policies that establish the existence of sound economic, environmental, and poverty reduction policies as the first factor or hurdle that must be crossed before a country receives regular lending resources. Transparent procedures to implement this policy are in place.*

ACCESS TO MDB RESOURCES: Governance Adequate for Program Success

Background

The Task Force encountered significant evidence that problems with borrower governance have often led to MDB program failures. However, the MDBs have been constrained in their response to these problems by occasional overly restrictive interpretations of their articles of agreement against consideration of noneconomic factors in their activities and by the reluctance of some of their executive directors to support a more active position on governance concerns. (The exception is the EBRD, which has a charter requirement to promote democratic governance.)

In addition, several aspects of MDB operations have combined to exert a negative impact on governance in their borrowers. The MDBs themselves generally have operated in a closed, top-down manner and traditionally have not challenged borrowing governments to follow more open and accountable practices as they consider policy changes and future investments.

Even when the MDBs have adopted policies calling for more inclusive procedures, such as consultation with project beneficiaries, the banks' method of implementing projects places the responsibility for doing this on the borrowing government. At most, the MDBs might ask for a report from the government on progress made. Numerous studies, especially in the area of resettlement and projects impacting on the environment, have noted that the banks have hesitated to press their client governments when questions were raised about whether they were fulfilling their responsibilities regarding such interactions.

Change Needed

The MDBs need to learn from past programs that did not work and clearly recognize that often the quality of governance sets limits on what can be accomplished in economic programs. For this reason, governance is relevant to all of their programs. Responsible stewardship of resources requires that they survey the obstacles to program and project success caused by governance problems before approving projects. Specifically, the MDBs should assess realistically the country environment regarding factors where there are key linkages between governance characteristics and economic results:

❐ Economic growth is unlikely unless investors, both domestic and foreign, have the incentive to invest that is provided by the rule of law, respect for property rights, fair enforcement and dispute settlement procedures, and containment of corruption.

❐ Effective government efforts to foster growth that is both broadly shared and environmentally sustainable and to invest in their own people are unlikely unless the government is accountable enough to minimize corruption and diversion of resources to low-priority uses.

❏ Governments are unlikely to have the responsiveness to their least powerful citizens needed for successful poverty reduction unless they have the incentive of some form of representative government under which popular support matters. Likewise, the rule of law and its fair enforcement protect the access of the poor to opportunities and markets and help to safeguard their property. In order to have effective real participation, which has been shown to be essential for many types of projects, proposed beneficiaries must be able to organize themselves, associate freely, make this their views known, and have an independent voice. Without these conditions, discussion of local participation is likely to be unrealistic.

In view of these linkages, the MDBs should see improving governance in all of these areas as a matter of their legitimate concern and consistent with their charters, in order to achieve their economic objectives.

> **RECOMMENDATION 2. Access to MDB Resources: Governance Adequate for Program Success.** The MDBs should more actively support improved governance as a means to improved economic growth and poverty reduction objectives by doing the following:
>
> • Making governance adequate for sustainable growth and poverty reduction a threshold test for receipt of loans. This would include enough accountability to contain corruption and diversion of resources, enough respect for law and its enforcement to permit growth, and enough of the attributes of representative government to make sustained improvement in the opportunities for the poor likely.
>
> • Taking a more proactive stance on governance in the course of normal activities. This would include especially checking on adherence to project covenants and bank policies and taking prompt and decisive action when violations occur.
>
> • Changing the MDBs' own operating modalities concerning transparency and open dialogue with diverse groups before programs are adopted so that the MDBs themselves become examples and forces for increased accountability. (This is discussed in detail in subsequent recommendations.)
>
> **BENCHMARK.** *Each MDB has adopted policies and procedures to look explicitly at the governance environment in each of its borrowers to determine whether it is adequate for the success of its programs, and these procedures are being implemented.*

ACCESS TO MDB RESOURCES: Graduation

Background

A cause for concern has long been the perception that few countries graduate or are expected to graduate soon from receipt of MDB resources.

Most of the MDBs have policies for moving borrowers from reliance on concessional to hard-window resources and then for graduating them from all lending. These policies tend to be complex, however, and the procedures for applying them obscure. In recent years countries have seldom been hailed as graduates, and those that were, such as Korea from the World Bank, often elicited surprise that they had not graduated earlier.

Change Needed

The Task Force concluded that graduation policies should be reviewed in a more active and transparent way than most of the MDBs have recently done.

The Task Force also thought that the MDBs should be seen by themselves, their borrowers, and their donors as transition instruments, assisting countries to move progressively away from the need for subsidized public resources of any type. When circumstances are appropriate, they should help borrowers structure projects to facilitate private financial participation as part of this transition. Even for countries that are not close to graduation thresholds, the MDBs should base their operations on the idea that their funding is time limited in order to reduce dependency on aid flows.

Some banks, such as the ADB, seem to be doing interesting thinking on their role as centers of regional cooperation and intellectual collaboration for countries that have graduated as borrowers.

> **RECOMMENDATION 3. Access to MDB Resources: Graduation.** Each MDB should have clear graduation criteria from each of its facilities, transparent procedures for applying them, and regular reviews of whether its graduation criteria remain adequate. All of these must be rigorously enforced.

> **BENCHMARK.** *Each MDB has conducted a thorough review of its graduation policies and means of applying them. At the end of this process, each MDB should have a clearly defined path by which borrowers are expected to progress to less concessional assistance and finally to reliance on domestic and commercial funding sources.*

USE OF MDB RESOURCES: Fast-Disbursing Lending to Facilitate Policy Reform

Background

A major way whereby MDBs and their shareholders have sought to deal with situations of inadequate borrower policies has been to provide fast-disbursing MDB funding conditioned on either macroeconomic or sectoral-policy changes. Although there have certainly been cases where such lending has been effective, the Task Force believed that in many instances MDB lending under these programs has not led to the desired results and in some cases has provided the resources to permit severely flawed policy regimes to be maintained. New forms of policy-based lending that provide funds for large local-currency expenditures related to policy reforms (e.g., severance pay for government workers, recapitalizing pension funds, paying local debts of government agencies) can substitute for domestic resource mobilization and unnecessarily add to borrowers' foreign debt.

Change Needed

In view of the overriding importance of a good policy framework and the occasional opportunities the MDBs have to provide important support to a regime already committed to reform, the Task Force concluded that the MDBs should continue lending to support policy reforms, but only in carefully specified circumstances. Because the country conditions under which these loans can be successful are quite rare and unpredictable, the MDBs should not plan for them in regular country or annual lending programs, which tend to create pressure to proceed even if the fragile conditions of likely success are not present. The net result should be a continued downward trend in the relative importance of such fast-disbursing loans as has been occurring in the MDBs during the 1990s, compared with the late 1980s.

> **RECOMMENDATION 4. Use of MDB Resources: Fast-Disbursing Lending to Facilitate Policy Reform.** The MDBs should be much more selective in the circumstances in which they approve fast-disbursing policy-based loans, lending only under the following circumstances:
>
> - The reforms are strongly supported and "owned" by the local government. The MDBs' staff, of course, has to judge whether the reform program is sound from an economic, social, and environmental standpoint.
>
> - Disbursement of the loan is closely linked to implementation of the reform program through requirements for prior actions and disbursement tranching, rather than relying on statements of intent. Substantial prior reform implementation also should proceed any MDB disbursements for expenditures related to reforms.

- The impact of policy reforms on various economic groups has been analyzed and considered.

For loans that are likely to have major local impact, the MDBs should encourage broad local discussion and debate about alternatives, including especially by doing their own preparatory work and analysis of the loan and its reform elements in a transparent process. (See Recommendation 14.)

BENCHMARK. *Each MDB has adopted revised guidelines for fast-disbursing lending along the lines discussed above, and the loans they approve reflect these guidelines.*

USE OF MDB RESOURCES: Avoiding Displacement of Private Funds

Background

Most of the MDBs have some kind of statement in their charter or policy framework that they should not displace private capital that is available on appropriate terms. However, most, except the EBRD, are quite vague on the criteria by which they judge whether alternative private terms are appropriate, and even more vague on the procedure they use to make this determination.

This is a more serious issue than it was in the past because private capital markets, both domestic and foreign, are evolving at such a rapid rate that a project that might not have been financeable from private sources a year ago, or even a few months previously, may now be able to attract private funding. Likewise, what constitutes appropriate terms is often a very complex question.

Change Needed

The MDBs should take additional steps to avoid competing with or displacing private funding, including in cases where private funding likely would be available if the borrower adopted appropriate policies. Especially, they should update their ability to respond to rapid changes in the domestic and foreign financial markets as to what funding is available.

The MDBs should make it clear that they will not support public-sector solutions when reasonable private alternatives are available. Obviously, cases where market failures or externalities make private funding impractical or undesirable should be exceptions, but the reason for the exception and why the private sector cannot deal with the problem should be made clear. At the same time, the MDBs should be more vigilant and active in opposing the creation of private monopolies, such as have been created when some state-owned enterprises in developing countries were privatized.

RECOMMENDATION 5. Use of MDB Resources: Avoiding Displacement of Private Funds. The MDBs need to have much clearer and more systematic policies to assure that they do not displace available private-sector funding (both domestic and foreign) or fund projects that the private sector would finance if borrowing governments adopted needed policy reforms. These policies need to be augmented by transparent procedures for applying them and staff incentives to support real change.

The MDBs also need to examine potentially commercially financeable sectors and announce plans to phase out funding for different types of projects in different situations by a given date. (The ADB has already done this in some countries and sectors.) This will help motivate countries to get their policies and regulatory frameworks in order to adapt to new circumstances.

BENCHMARK. Each MDB has put in place clear policies on non-displacement of private funds (with needed caveats for exceptions under carefully defined conditions) and transparent procedures to ensure their application. The MDBs in more-developed regions have formulated and announced plans for phasing out over a reasonable period funding for sectors and types of projects most likely to attract commercial funding.

USE OF MDB RESOURCES: Financial Support for Private Projects

Background

For years the MDBs have debated whether, to what extent, and how they should directly support projects developed by the private sector and containing substantial private investment. Given the dramatic changes in attitudes toward the private sector in many countries and in the potential reach of capital market vehicles, this question is now even more critical.

It looms especially large for the new private infrastructure projects that are being proposed for many countries. MDBs were designed to meet the traditional needs of public-sector infrastructure finance in developing countries. Long-term, publicly guaranteed, foreign-exchange loans seemed well suited to the needs of the public power companies, port authorities, and highway administrations of the developing world. In addition, construction of such infrastructure seemed relatively straightforward, with selection of a good construction contractor and supervising engineering firm expected to produce acceptable results. MDB staff only needed to review project designs, supervise the bidding process, and check requests for payment.

Over the last several years, however, the problems with this model and the external changes that are making it obsolete in many areas have become evident. Some kinds of large infrastructure projects often caused severe environmental problems. Many of the public-sector operating companies proved unable to operate the infrastructure efficiently or, despite repeated conditionality in MDB loans, to develop pricing and maintenance systems that could make it sustainable. The World Bank's 1994 *World Development Report* estimated that developing countries could save $123 billion annually in the power, water, and railways sectors alone by reducing subsidies and making technical efficiency improvements.

A 1996 World Bank Operations Evaluation Department (OED) Report described the results of Bank lending for electric power in Africa:

> Since 1978 the Bank has invested $2.3 billion and attracted $2.5 billion in cofinancing for power in Sub-Saharan Africa. Physical implementation has been no worse in Sub-Saharan Africa than in other regions. But the Bank's impact on the technical and commercial performance of the sector has been limited.... Nearly two thirds (of forty-one projects studied in twenty-two countries) were rated uncertain or unlikely to sustain their benefits.... Borrowers' compliance with covenants was negligible in more than 60 percent of cases. Compliance was especially weak on important financial covenants—for collection of accounts receivable, approval of tariff increases, and the financial return on fixed assets.... Bank assistance achieved very little improvement in the technical and commercial efficiency of the power utilities.... With few exceptions— Burundi, Côte d'Ivoire, Ghana, Guinea, and Nigeria among them—the provision of electricity to low income households was pursued weakly or not at all.
>
> Africa's shortages of skilled people have posed serious difficulties, but the greater obstacles have been institutional: government interference in power companies' day-to-day operations, power companies' inability to make and enforce decisions on manpower, bill collection, and procurement of parts, and stubborn political opposition to justified tariff increases.[6]

As these problems were surfacing, a few pioneering developing countries and companies (many of them American) found that they could build and operate infrastructure in developing countries more cheaply and with much greater efficiency than the old public monopolies. They were assisted by new technologies, especially in power, transport, and telecommunications, that made it possible to unbundle giant systems into smaller entities that private companies were more able to finance.

The new private infrastructure is far less dependent on public funding, either from developing-country governments or from international agencies, than were the old public projects. This makes it appealing to developing-country governments that are facing massive demand increases for infrastructure to support desired economic growth rates. However, a debate has emerged about whether or how the MDBs should provide guarantees or other measures to support what are usually fairly small pieces of these large private infrastructure projects. The question is whether the MDBs have a comparative advantage and whether it is in the public

---

6. World Bank, Operations Evaluation Department (OED), "Bank Lending for Electric Power in Africa: Time for a Reappraisal," *OED Précis* (Washington, D.C.: World Bank, January 1996), 1–2.

interest for them to help reduce the political risk taken by some of the private parties in these projects.

Purpose of MDB involvement. Because the MDBs are publicly supported institutions, it is widely agreed that they should put resources into particular private projects only to achieve important public-policy objectives. In general, the best way for the MDB to decide if a private project should be seen as a priority would be to look at it in the context of the institution's lending strategy for that country to help achieve priority development objectives and weigh to what degree it would help achieve them.

Private projects should meet regular MDB criteria in public-policy areas such as environmental sustainability. As well, the MDBs may be in a good position to encourage creative innovations in the form of joint ventures between for-profit and not-for-profit entities to support development objectives. In some cases, the MDBs may have unique capabilities to support these innovations, serving as links between disparate groups and disseminating information on best practices in these cutting-edge partnerships. For example, the World Bank Group, especially IFC and GEF, has recently initiated several mechanisms to encourage private financing of enterprises in the areas of energy efficiency, renewable energy, and biodiversity.

Extent of MDB involvement. Normally, for sound projects, equity and short-term debt financing are readily available. The part of the financing package for which MDB guarantees or "credit enhancements" are sought is the long-term debt portion. Likewise, commercial risks generally can be borne commercially, but MDB or other official insurance or guarantees are sought to cover the political risk of future developing-country governments' failing to honor their commitments. Usually the portion of project costs that the MDB would be asked to cover would be fairly small, and would involve much less MDB funding than old-style MDB loans to public entities to construct infrastructure.

The argument is that the MDBs as international public agencies can increase the comfort of developing-country governments and their citizens that a private infrastructure deal is fair to them, and reassure investors that they will have a powerful ally on their side if the host government arbitrarily reneges on its part of the deal. This reassurance, it is contended, can make the riskier parts of the project financing package available, when otherwise they would not be, or available on better terms, which would reduce the price of the service to the consumer. The contention is that the public benefit of the private project being undertaken, without having to make full provision for the political risk of bad behavior by the host government for 20–30 years into the future, justifies the MDB involvement. Otherwise, for the first few private projects in a risky market, private lenders would charge such high interest rates that user fees would have to be pushed up beyond tolerable levels to cover project financing costs.

The opposing argument is that international capital markets are artificially distorted by these programs in favor of excessively risky and lower-priority projects.

Currently the MDBs have a wide variety of programs to support private projects directly. However, these programs tend to be very small in comparison to total MDB lending and certainly to the size of most private infrastructure projects, hedged in by many restrictions, and fragmented among MDB organizational units. (The exception is the newer EBRD, which devotes over 75 percent of its lending to direct support for private projects.) These programs and their limitations are described in Appendix B.

Modality in the World Bank Group. In addition to debate about how much the MDBs should directly support private-sector projects, there is substantial disagreement about the best institutional modality for the World Bank Group to utilize to provide such support. Currently the World Bank itself, as well as its IFC and MIGA affiliates, all have programs for direct support to private-sector projects.

If expansion of World Bank Group private-sector financing is envisaged or if it is believed that greater efficiency and coherence is needed at current program levels, usually one of two means is contemplated:

❑   Within the World Bank Group, select IFC and MIGA as the most suitable vehicles for private-sector catalytic programs. Transfer responsibility for executing major private-sector transactions (especially the guarantee program), along with staff and needed capital, to IFC/MIGA, probably through a subordinated loan from the IBRD.

❑   Open up the possibility for the World Bank itself to play a less restricted role in private-sector catalytic efforts by removing the charter requirement for a government guarantee.

These two options need not be alternatives. It might be possible to proceed immediately with the first option while beginning efforts to achieve the second. Some believe that changing the World Bank's charter to permit lending to private borrowers without a government guarantee could be very useful in other areas, because it would open up other possible channels for MDB–civil society partnerships without the requirement for a government intermediary role.

Change Needed

Purpose of MDB involvement. The MDBs should improve their country lending strategies to analyze clearly development constraints facing their borrowers and determine priority investments taking into account what other donors may be planning. These strategies should factor in possible private-sector projects that the development bank might support, analyzing their relative priority on the basis of public-policy objectives compared with alternative uses of funds. Private-sector affiliates should fully participate in this process and should be guided by its results.

> **RECOMMENDATION 6a. Use of MDB Resources: Financial Support for Private Projects—Public Purpose.** Any private projects chosen for direct support should be selected by the MDBs through their country strategy process on the basis of effective contribution to development objectives.

The MDBs need to have clear means by which they apply their normal project standards (e.g., environmental standards) to private-sector projects they support.

BENCHMARK. Each MDB has such processes and procedures and is enforcing them.

Extent of MDB involvement. The Task Force looked at a number of possibilities concerning the MDBs' role vis-à-vis private projects in developing countries. It was recognized, however, that several of these formulations would involve a substantial expansion of the MDBs' role and that few MDB personnel have extensive experience in private-sector lending. (An increase in overall MDB lending would not necessarily be entailed, however, because the increase in private-sector support could take place in conjunction with a decline in lending for public-sector infrastructure projects.) Therefore, many Task Force members believe that such steps should only be undertaken after reforms in the MDBs themselves have been made.

RECOMMENDATION 6b. Use of MDB Resources: Financial Support for Private Projects—Options Concerning Extent and Nature of Direct MDB Support for Private Projects.

OPTION 1. Continue Existing Type and Level of Support.

- Based on the view that there is no compelling need for expansion in this type of program. Also, expanding the MDBs' role in this area would require staff skills the MDBs lack and contradict calls for them to focus on fewer priorities.

- Would maintain current programs in existing institutional arrangements.

- Programs would continue to grow at current rates (10–15 percent a year for IFC and MIGA, some growth in other guarantee programs).

- Process improvements now under way (such as moves toward one-stop shopping for private project sponsors at the World Bank) would continue.

- Efforts would continue to ensure that private-sector projects meet the same standards as other MDB projects, especially in the area of environmental standards.

OPTION 2. Abolish MDB Programs to Support Private Projects Directly.

- Based on the view that if investors judge a project to be viable, they will invest in it at the right price. The market's judgment on a project's viability is more trustworthy than that of political institutions such as the MDBs. The refusal of the market to fund projects would be a powerful incentive for governments to adopt and maintain reform programs.

- Would call for phaseout of most of the EBRD's programs (75 percent) and virtually all of IFC's and MIGA's.

- Would abolish smaller programs in the IBRD and the other three regional banks.

OPTION 3. Revised Program for Private-Sector Funding, Small Version.

Strengthened Conditions.

MDBs would provide direct support to private projects in a country only after they have negotiated a Framework Agreement with the country. (The existence of such an agreement should reduce the delays that now occur as each MDB project officer scrutinizes the issues individually.) The Agreement would cover

- economic policies and policies regarding foreign investment necessary for the success of private projects;

- sector policies and regulatory requirements for specified sectors; and

- common standards for private investors concerning public-policy issues (e.g., environment).

Rapid and Defined Graduation From Support for Private Projects.

MDBs would clearly specify how they plan to phase out support soon for private projects in the country and sector. This plan could call for phaseout in a defined time period, after a fixed number of transactions, or when some other clearly specified and easily monitorable condition is met. These conditions should be defined in such a way as to provide an incentive for the country to move as fast as possible to end the need for MDB direct support for private investments and/or provide a disincentive for delay.

Both the Framework Agreement (the product of negotiation between the MDB and the country) and the MDB's graduation plan for private-sector finance (an MDB document) would be public documents. These agreements should make it clear what countries and sectors are "open for business" for private projects, thus eliminating some current reasons for delays in making decisions on private projects.

More Flexible Program.

This option would call for the lessening or potentially the removal of some of the barriers to funding private-sector projects. Specifically:

- Either the World Bank's requirement for a government guarantee in all cases would be relaxed, or capital would be transferred to IFC so that, if needed, it could play a larger role, especially in guarantees for large projects. Current IFC policy limits on financing per project and per country would be relaxed.

- MIGA would receive a modest capital increase by means of a capital transfer from the IBRD so that it could continue its program and expand somewhat its country and project limits. It would be permitted to provide political-risk coverage for loans not associated with equity investments. If it appeared necessary to supplement the IBRD's or IFC's guarantee program, MIGA would be urged to broaden its breach-of-contract coverage, which is currently very restricted.

- The artificial restrictions on the percentages of the regional banks' (except for the EBRD, which has no restrictions) lending programs (or guarantees) that could go to private projects without a government guarantee would be relaxed. This decision would be left to each MDB's management on the basis of country and project circumstances.

- MDBs should fill some staff vacancies with individuals possessing specialized financial skills. If the MDBs play a broader role in supporting specific transactions, they will need staff with business and financial sophistication comparable to that of the firms with which they deal.

OPTION 4. Revised Program for Private-Sector Funding, Expanded Version.

Strengthened Conditions.

Same as with Option 3.

Defined Graduation.

The approach would be the same as under Option 3, but based on the view that progress toward improved creditworthiness often is not linear, and it is in everyone's interest to allow a somewhat longer time period before the MDBs cease providing limited support to private projects in specific countries and sectors, so that reforms are solidified and reversals that would undercut the expansion of private funding are avoided. However, the same process of a defined, publicly known graduation plan would be followed.

More Flexible and Active Program to Support Private-Sector Alternatives.

- This option would surpass the changes called for in Option 3 in that the MDBs would go beyond removing restrictions that currently limit their support for private projects to engaging in proactive efforts to find and support such projects. They would be more active in seeking to devise private-sector options in situations where public-sector solutions have not worked.

- Although the funding devoted to support of private projects would depend on country and private-sector choices, it would probably be significantly larger than under Option 3, with the increase probably coming at the expense of public-sector infrastructure.

Approximately 16 percent of the Task Force members support Option 1, 11 percent Option 2, 40 percent Option 3 or a variant of it calling for a small expansion in private programs over a longer time period, and 33 percent Option 4.

Modality in the World Bank Group. If support for private projects is continued, many think that the Bank Group should make a clearer decision about the main locus of direct support for private projects. The current situation with IFC, MIGA, several central World Bank units, and the regular Bank country operating departments involved in support for the private sector invites turf battles and probably does not lead to the best use of scarce private-sector and financial-market expertise. (The creation of a managing director for the private sector has improved coordination but may not be able to overcome the inherent problems and inefficiencies of having so many organizational units doing closely related things.) It certainly would be easier for World Bank Country Assistance Strategies to look at the relative priority of private-sector projects if the mandate to consider private-sector projects and issues were not so fragmented.

> **RECOMMENDATION 6c. Use of MDB Resources: Financial Support for Private Projects—Modality in the World Bank Group.** A decision should be made about the major center of responsibility for direct World Bank support of private projects. This center could be either of the following:
>
> - An expanded IFC, possibly combined with MIGA, which also would have responsibility for executing most other private-sector projects (especially the private-sector guarantee program currently in the World Bank). Appropriate staff and needed capital could be transferred from the World Bank (in the case of capital through a subordinated loan from the IBRD).
>
> - The World Bank itself, with IFC and MIGA brought into a closer organizational relationship with an expanded World Bank private-transactions unit. This would involve a change in the World Bank Articles of Agreement to permit lending without a government guarantee.
>
> **BENCHMARK.** *A decision on the focus of responsibility for private-sector transactions in the World Bank Group has been made and is being implemented.*

These changes could be pursued sequentially, especially if it is believed, as many do, that changing the World Bank's charter would take a long time. To the extent that Task Force members saw these as alternatives, at least for immediate action, the group was nearly evenly divided, with 53 percent supporting the IFC-led option, and 47 percent preferring the IBRD-led option.

USE OF MDB RESOURCES: Building on a Country Commitment to Poverty Reduction

Background

MDB funding consistently is sought by the banks themselves and U.S. administrations on the grounds that it reduces poverty and over time improves the lives of the disadvantaged in developing countries. (This does not apply to the EBRD, which has been given a different mandate by its shareholders.)

A major problem in making this a reality is the lack of commitment to this objective on the part of many developing-country governments and ruling elites. In most developing countries, poverty is a massive problem that cannot be dealt with comprehensively by small efforts. Generally, the amount of resources an MDB can bring to bear on the problem is only a tiny fraction of what is needed.

There are several ways an MDB can try to deal with this problem. One, which has often been attempted, is to direct the MDB's own funding into projects that are aimed at helping the poor, try to get some borrowing-government money for the same program on a pari passu basis, and hope that the lack-of-government-commitment problem will be resolved during project execution and that the government will decide to sustain and even replicate the program with its own funds. Unfortunately, when there is a failure of local commitment, usually this optimistic scenario does not transpire. The most such programs do is improve the lives of some poor people (if benefits are not hijacked by richer groups) while the project is ongoing. When the MDB funding ceases, the programs are unlikely to be sustained or used as a model for broader-scale replication.

This approach also has the downside of allowing the uncommitted government to create the illusion that it is doing something for its poor, and helping to hold at bay both internal and external pressures for real change. Likewise, taxpayers in donor countries are led to expect that their money is helping to reduce poverty—an expectation that is unlikely to be fulfilled, at least in terms of lasting progress, thus possibly leading to further cynicism about the value of international aid.

Change Needed

The Task Force thinks that the MDBs should establish a higher minimum level of demonstrated commitment from the borrowing-country government to resolving its own poverty problems as part of the threshold test of policy adequacy for receiving MDB funding. This requirement is also justified on the grounds of the importance of government policies in this area to stable, long-term growth and integration into the international economy.

As to modalities to implement this, mechanistic formulas (as to percent of budget spent on social sectors, etc.) usually do not capture fully the differences among countries or the complexities of individual situations. Therefore, the MDBs should draw up types of criteria they will consider, such as where the domestic tax burden falls, whether social services for the poor receive a fair share of funding, the effect of government regulations on the poor (including their property rights), and barriers to entry and operation of small and labor-using businesses and microenterprises. The MDBs may also want to consider the direction of change and the nature and quality of the dialogue within the country that leads to policy formulation to judge whether the interests of the poor are adequately reflected.

In making final decisions on whether country commitment to poverty reduction is adequate, the MDBs will need to rely on the best professional judgment of their senior managers. These decisions should be made public, and the basis for them should be transparent. To assist with these judgments, the MDBs will need to devote increased analytical effort to looking at how various policy choices affect different economic and social groups.

> **RECOMMENDATION 7. Use of MDB Resources: Building on a Country Commitment to Poverty Reduction.** The MDBs (except for the EBRD) should adopt policies making a serious demonstrated commitment to poverty reduction a requirement for an MDB loan program.

> **BENCHMARK.** *Each MDB (except the EBRD) has put in place such a policy and transparent procedures for applying it.*

USE OF MDB RESOURCES: Increasing the Productive Capacity of the Poor

There is much evidence that economic growth is absolutely necessary for poverty reduction. If the poor are to benefit from this growth, however, they must have the opportunity to access assets and be empowered to use them productively. Therefore, the centerpiece of poverty reduction strategies needs to be sustainable means to link the poor with productive assets, and then to tie small-scale productive activities through freely competitive linkages to the larger private market, so that they can prosper and expand.

The focus of this section is on direct MDB efforts to create these links. Such efforts include investing in the human capital of the poor (education, health, and family planning services) and their access to other productive assets. Many programs in these areas have been funded by governments and aid providers, including the MDBs. The Task Force focused much attention on what types of activities were suited to the products and services the MDBs can provide, and on the most effective ways to make those products available. This recommendation looks at what activities the MDBs should emphasize, in light of the type of resources and products they can make available. (Many aspects of this recommendation do not apply to the EBRD in view of its distinct mandate.)

Small Business and Microenterprise

Background. Small business and microenterprise is one of the most important ways in which both the urban and rural poor in developing countries make their living. In many areas of the developing world, microenterprises provide over half the employment for the working poor. Evidence from some developing countries that more than 50 percent of medium-sized firms originated as microenterprises underlines the importance of this sector for broader economic growth. Small firms also may make available goods and services (including environmentally beneficial technologies) needed by poor or isolated groups.

For many years, there have been programs managed and funded by governments, and sometimes supported by aid donors (including the MDBs), to provide credit and other assistance to these small businesses. Most of these programs were not sustainable due either to uneconomic credit terms or to poor repayment records. Because these programs were run by governments, they were perceived to be (and often were) subsidies to particular groups, with little attention paid to financial sustainability. In addition, larger enterprises succeeded in appropriating the subsidized credit even though it was intended for poorer groups. Many of these programs have been discontinued or significantly reduced in size.

In recent years, a new generation of microfinance institutions has appeared, operated by private-sector groups such as NGOs, credit unions, and some commercial banks. These institutions charge market interest rates and utilize sound accounting and management systems to help them achieve financial sustainability. They have also achieved high repayment rates through peer pressure lending—the use of community guarantees. A number of these institutions have evolved as financial intermediaries supporting a network of community financial entities. In 1993–1994, NGOs of this type reported a doubling of their aggregate loan portfolio.

These new institutions that support microenterprise remain relatively fragile, however, reaching about 13 million of the estimated 200 million low-income microentrepreneurs in the developing world.

The challenge for the MDBs is to help these fragile but promising new organizations to become a significant force to improve opportunities for the poor without either overwhelming their capacities or replicating the mistakes of government-supported subsidized credit systems, many of which were funded by the MDBs.

Change needed. The MDBs should strongly support this new type of microenterprise finance system, but in ways different from their traditional large loans for onlending to small and microentrepreneurs. They should focus on the following:

❏ The MDBs should make improvements in local laws and regulations that hamper small and microenterprises a major priority in their discussions of government policies. These measures include changes in taxation policy, property rights (including women's ability to own property), intellectual property rights, barriers to starting new businesses, and laws governing banking and usury. Bringing about the establishment of a legal and regulatory framework that supports micro- and small enterprises is often quite difficult. The maze of rules that hampers small operations is often intricate, and changing regulations and burdensome procedures, as well as ensuring that changes are enforced, can be as important as major policy changes. In addition, borrowing governments often perceive small business to be unimportant to their economic plans or are reluctant to risk the opposition of local elites, who see new start-ups as competition. The magnitude of the regulatory burden faced by entrepreneurs is exemplified by the situation in Mexico, where it is said that establishing a legal microenterprise requires 416 different permits and a wait of at least nine months.[7]

❑ The MDBs should use their ability to encourage dialogue between and work with different groups to integrate the poor into the country's formal financial system. MDBs should work with governments to remove impediments and create incentives for commercial banks to provide services to the intermediaries (NGOs, credit unions, community-based associations) to establish linkages between microenterprise systems and the commercial financial sector.

❑ The MDBs can help to develop the capacities of international and national privately controlled wholesalers of microfinance to help these systems "scale up" in a cost-effective and responsible way. This involves helping them to develop common accounting, outreach, and management information systems and helping to train skilled managers.

These activities require relatively small amounts of MDB financial resources, but all are well suited to the MDBs' comparative advantages in influencing borrower governments, in bringing together diverse groups, and in designing ways to replicate successful small programs. What would be needed, however, is for the MDBs to assign microenterprise policy reform, linkage to the commercial sector, and capacity building much higher priority in their dialogues with governments and the commercial sector.

The MDBs and other official donors are currently providing some support to these institutions, but their approach has not been consistent or focused. In response to this, the World Bank and many other donors helped to create the Consultative Group to Assist the Poorest (CGAP) to coordinate and disseminate lessons from the various programs. It is not clear, however, that the CGAP members are giving this group the degree of high-level attention and leadership that is needed to create coordinated and streamlined capacity-building efforts that will enable the microenterprise wholesale institutions to achieve economies of scale and reach a more significant number of poor people.

As for funding for capacity building, it is advantageous if the MDBs can make available small amounts of grant funding for technical assistance and start-up costs or make small loans for seed capital directly to the private wholesale entities. When they cannot, due to lack of grant funding capability or the need for a government guarantee on loans, at times the MDBs have been able to create pass-through organizations, which can receive a government-guaranteed loan but are structured to be independent enough from government interference not to encounter the kinds of problems that occurred with government-run microcredit programs.

---

7.   Statistic provided in a speech by Roberto Salinas-León, executive director of the Center for Free Enterprise Research (CISLE) in Mexico City, given at the Cato Institute, Washington, D.C., November 21, 1996.

Regarding whether the MDBs themselves should provide loans for onlending to small enterprises and microenterprises, in many cases it appears that more money for actual onlending for microenterprise credit is not needed in view of current institutional capacity constraints. The lessons of experience argue strongly against providing expanded resources for onlending before intermediaries demonstrate the capacity to manage larger operations in a financially sustainable way, and it may not be advantageous for developing countries to incur foreign currency debt for microenterprise onlending. In any case, only those MDBs that have financial products suited to microcredit (loans that can go directly to the private sector) and close knowledge of experienced microcredit intermediary institutions should be involved in providing such funding. If they make such loans, the banks should build on the lessons from other MDB credit endeavors, which generally underestimated risks and placed more emphasis on funneling money to recipients than worrying about the sustainability of the financial institution. Because the amount of money donors can provide is so small in comparison to the scale of the potential, achieving institutional financial sustainability must be a central objective.

RECOMMENDATION 8a. Use of MDB Resources: Increasing the Productive Capacity of the Poor—Small Business and Microenterprise. The MDBs should take a much stronger leadership position in helping to establish the building blocks for successful microenterprise activities through the following:

- strong dialogue with governments to remove policy and regulatory obstacles to small and micro business;

- efforts to foster linkages between the grassroots infrastructure of the informal economy and commercial financial institutions, building on the MDBs' ability to interact with governments, large-scale financial institutions, and microenterprise groups;

- leadership in coordinating scaled-up capacity building for microenterprise intermediary institutions.

The type of initiative the Task Force recommends would be untypical for an MDB in that it would be focused not on the expenditure of large amounts of MDB financial resources but on greater use of MDB policy leverage, leadership, organizational skills, and ability to forge linkages among diverse groups. It would require investment of senior MDB managements' time and political credibility in support of small entrepreneurs.

BENCHMARK. *Each MDB has analyzed its possible contributions to small and microenterprise and produced a comprehensive strategy consistent with the needs of the sector and its own capabilities. Several of the MDBs (whose mandates and operating environments are suitable) have initiated programs that are effectively removing obstacles for scaled-up and more significant microenterprise programs.*

Making Markets Work for the Rural Poor

Background. Nearly three-fourths of the world's poor still live in rural areas. Many of these areas remain heavily dependent on agriculture, which led one speaker at a Task Force meeting to note that if "you grow a country without developing agriculture, you leave most of the people out."[8] In addition, World Bank Operations Evaluations Department studies found that faster poverty reduction is correlated with dynamic agricultural growth rates and that in no case did poverty measures decline when agriculture growth was slow.[9]

However, most of the MDBs, as well as many other aid agencies, have experienced many failed agricultural projects—generally large-scale, expensive state-dominated schemes. Some of the MDBs have reacted to the problems in their agricultural loan portfolio by reducing their attention to the sector.

Change needed. The MDBs should change their approach in light of lessons learned in past projects and especially to take account of changes in international agricultural prices and markets and the improved policy environment prevailing in some developing countries. In particular, they should develop their expertise to help countries achieve the transformations needed to make trade-driven and market-led development work for small agricultural producers. Not only could this contribute to equitable growth, but it can also safeguard the natural resource base, improve nutrition, and contribute to decentralization of population and services and improved local governance. When small farmers have the opportunity to increase their incomes through sustainable practices, they are less likely to migrate to areas where the land cannot sustain farming or to already overcrowded urban slums.

❏ In many cases, the most important thing the MDBs can do is to support national economic policies conducive to market-led, environmentally sustainable growth in the agricultural sector, which is likely to benefit small farmers. In cases (especially instances of subsidized competition from foreign producers) where small farmers are not likely to be able to make an adequate living under market-determined conditions, the MDBs need to provide analytical support to devise solutions appropriate to the particular situation that move away from continued subsidies or trade barriers in a specific time frame but in the meantime provide prior assistance to the small farmers in making a transition to alternative crops or other occupations, if an internationally negotiated solution to subsidized foreign competition is not possible.

❏ The land-tenure situation, the functioning of competitive rural land markets, and the safeguarding of property rights (including fair application and enforcement of the law concerning land rights in rural areas) have a major

---

8.   John Mellor, former director of the International Food Policy Research Institute, at a CSIS Task Force working group meeting, Washington, D.C., July 26, 1996.

9.   Robert Picciotto, director general of the World Bank Operations Evaluation Department, presentation to the Religious Working Group of the World Bank-IMF, August 8, 1996.

impact on the ability of the rural poor to respond to market opportunities. Currently, rural producers are constrained due to insecure titles and unreliable land markets and titling services. In the past, however, attempts by outside funders to support programs to improve the land situation of small farmers have sometimes resulted both in the creation of uneconomic collective schemes that further impoverished the farmers or in the perversion of individual titling programs by local power brokers (with local elites usurping what land rights the poor had had).

In many cases, individual land ownership creates incentives for increased production and good environmental practices. However, this may not be true in societies where, by long-standing tradition or customary right, land is used and held by extended families, clans, or other traditional groups. Thus, decisions about conversions of group title to individual title should be made by the free choice of the people affected. Any MDB efforts to improve the land tenure situation or the functioning of land markets must be designed with great attention to the details of the local situation and must be accompanied by very close monitoring of its implementation by experienced and disinterested parties. If this is not possible, MDB programs can easily be undermined by the unequal power and income relationships that prevail in many rural areas. As Alan Durning has noted, "Almost without exception, the net effect of state land policies has been to drastically curtail common property resources open to the poor, without expanding their private property resources commensurately."[10]

One Task Force member noted that in this area "the devil is truly in the details"; for any MDB program to be successful, the institution must thoroughly understand the local reality, fully grasp the motivations of all the groups with which it works, and watch the situation on the ground carefully all the way through the project.[11]

❏ The MDBs should continue their investments in rural roads and transportation systems that take advantage of the MDBs' comparative advantage in providing foreign exchange for investments that are unlikely to attract private capital. In rural areas where many small farmers are currently operating and where land is suitable for sustainable agriculture, few investments can do as much as transportation infrastructure to help small farmers secure a productive role in a competitive market economy. However, the MDBs need to pay greater attention than in the past to the consequences of new roads that open up fragile land to potential environmental degradation, and the MDBs should work much more intensively with local residents to set up local systems to maintain the roads. (See Recommendation 11a on local participation.)

10. Alan Durning, *Poverty and the Environment: Reversing the Downward Spiral*, Worldwatch Paper 92 (Washington, D.C.: Worldwatch Institute, November 1989), 47.

11. David Bathrick, former president of the Association for International Agriculture and Rural Development, at a CSIS Task Force meeting, Washington, D.C., September 25, 1996.

❏ The MDBs should take advantage of their technical knowledge and global experience to help borrowing countries expand their attention to natural resource management and agricultural-related environmental and public-health concerns. These include soil degradation and related water-quality problems as well as water management, worker safety, and consumer health issues related to chemical applications and residues.

❏ Throughout the developing world, many of the government monopolies that supplied farm inputs and marketed farm produce have been disbanded or are giving way to private alternatives. In many cases, however, the new private input supply, technology development, and marketing systems are not yet fully in place (or in some cases uncompetitive private monopolies have emerged) so they do not efficiently reach small farmers. In addition, post-harvest and value-added processes (e.g., refrigeration, packing, grading and sorting) may need to be introduced, and input and product marketing and management skills may need to be acquired. These problems and delays in the path to fully private systems are location specific and changing. If the MDBs could develop the needed local knowledge and entrepreneurship, they could help provide the impetus (via small-scale training efforts or seed money for new ventures) for strategic partnerships among producer groups, the for-profit private sector, NGOs, and local governments to find solutions to these discontinuities. This kind of effort would also require the flexibility to develop small, agile projects, often in collaboration with local partners.

❏ Although more agricultural research is being done in the private sector or is supported by more-specialized donors, in some cases a "public good" rationale may still impel the MDBs to support selectively some work of reformed national agricultural research and outreach entities, including for production technologies that permit poor farmers to cultivate land intensively and sustainably rather than continue extensive farming that harms the land.

> **RECOMMENDATION 8b. Use of MDB Resources: Increasing the Productive Capacity of the Poor—Making Markets Work for the Rural Poor.** Commensurate with their capabilities, the MDBs should support measures to make the new trade and market-led agricultural development system work well for the rural poor.
>
> **BENCHMARK.** *Each MDB has prepared a comprehensive strategy based on its own capabilities to help its borrowers and especially their small producers adapt to the changes brought by globalization and other trends in international agricultural markets. These strategies are being implemented.*

Selected High-Priority Investments in Human Capital

Background. The establishment of efficient and effective programs to develop the human capital of the poor through education, health, and family planning are critical elements for sustainable economic growth and poverty reduction. It has been shown that investments in effective programs of this type often have extremely high rates of return. Because this is so important, the Task Force thinks efforts by potential borrowers to mobilize their own resources and allocate a reasonable amount of them to these programs, compared with other expenditures, should be an important element in deciding whether the country's policy framework is adequate to merit MDB funding.

Challenges for MDBs presented by human capital programs. The importance of these programs does not mean that they are always suited to MDB funding. Human resource development programs present a number of challenges for the MDBs:

☐ *Mismatch between type of resources MDBs can make available and the needs of some social programs.* Often the budgets of social-sector programs are heavily weighted toward local-currency expenditures and recurring costs (e.g., salaries of teachers and health personnel). Due to the MDBs' own mechanism for raising funds, almost all of their resources must go out as loans that must be repaid in convertible currency. All but the poorest countries must repay these loans on near-market terms (fairly high interest rates, short grace periods). Therefore, borrowing countries and the MDBs should be selective about what kinds of social investments they fund with these expensive resources that add to borrowers' foreign debt service burdens. As has become clear as the banks grapple with the problem of low-income country debt, even very concessional loans build repayment obligations surprisingly quickly.

☐ *Need to avoid the temptation to substitute for local resource mobilization.* Because social investments are seen as having such high priority for MDBs, there is a temptation for borrowing governments either to avoid mobilizing resources locally or to use them for lower-priority expenditures. Programs that do not have much borrower-government commitment often are not sustained once external resources have been exhausted.

Some social-sector reform programs may need large onetime local-currency expenditures for such things as severance pay for redundant workers or the recapitalization of pension funds. Funding these expenditures may be particularly tempting for an MDB that wishes to show a large volume of lending for social programs. From the borrower's perspective, however, it may not make sense to incur foreign debt for such costs. Likewise, from the standpoint of MDB program effectiveness, the borrower's lack of ability to mobilize domestic resources for these items may augur badly for the sustainability of reform programs.

❏ *Improving management of large and scattered national programs that may have a poor track record.* Another big challenge for the MDBs posed by this type of project is an operational one. A recent World Bank report, *Getting Results in the Social Sectors*, spelled out this challenge:

> The social sectors in general and some Bank supported projects in particular, entail a high degree of decentralization. Education and health systems typically consist of thousands of schools and clinics, with numerous entities involved, right down to local neighborhood committees. Projects, responding to the special needs these arrangements imply, sometimes contain large numbers of subprojects administered by disparate executing institutions. Social funds are one among several manifestations of this decentralized character, the antithesis of earlier Bank projects where one central ministry made all the decisions. The growing importance of participatory approaches, with outreach to beneficiaries and civil society broadly, has heightened the complexity of interactions required.
>
> To accommodate these needs effectively, projects need to adopt features that have traditionally not been common in Bank projects. One such feature is a focus on ensuring that the client country's institutional structure for overseeing implementation of a highly decentralized initiative is up to the task.[12]

Programs of this nature require both detailed knowledge of local situations and the ability to monitor a complex maze of local activities to see both if program objectives are being met and if the poor are benefiting as intended. The MDBs need to be able to meet these requirements in order to fulfill their objectives in this type of project. How the MDBs can change their operating systems to better face this challenge is discussed in the section on MDB Operations (Recommendations 9–13).

❏ *Improving social-sector policies: need for many sequential changes that may challenge vested interests.* The fourth challenge is presented by the projects some MDBs have begun to do, namely policy-based nonprojectized lending in the social sectors. Recommendation 4 discussed the obstacles that have hampered other MDB policy-based lending. In many respects, the problems presented by projects to provide funding for social-sector reform are even more difficult. Policy reforms are often opposed by powerful vested interests, and the changes required involve many small but important steps over a prolonged period (e.g., improving performance of teachers in poor areas, changing patterns of resource allocation in favor of primary health care). Even more so than in other areas, there are no "quick fixes" in reforming social-sector programs. Compared with other policy-based lending, it may be more important to have a solid track record of

---

12. World Bank Human Capital Department, Human Capital Development Vice Presidency, *Getting Results in the Social Sectors* (Washington, D.C.: World Bank, January 16, 1996), 23.

already implemented reforms before providing funding in the social sectors. Local ownership of reforms remains a necessity, and a thorough distributional analysis of the impact of reforms on various groups is also important.

> **RECOMMENDATION 8c. Use of MDB Resources: Increasing the Productive Capacity of the Poor—Selected High-Priority Investments in Human Capital.** An MDB should fund social-sector programs when
>
> - the MDB's financial product is suited to the need of the project and appropriate for the country's circumstances;
>
> - MDB involvement is not substituting for needed resource mobilization by the country or enabling the country to make lower-priority use of its own resources, and the project is likely to be sustained by the borrower after MDB funds are disbursed; and
>
> - the MDB has the capability to do the more time-consuming project preparatory work and careful local monitoring.
>
> - The MDBs should do policy-based lending in the social sectors only if the reforms are locally owned and disbursement of funds is tied to actual implementation of reforms.
>
> **BENCHMARK.** *Each MDB (except the EBRD, which does not do this type of project) has reviewed its social-sector portfolio and policies and addressed how it can meet the challenges posed by lending in these sectors, where the policy and management challenges are great and normal MDB operating modalities are not adequate.*

MDB OPERATIONS

In addition to looking at what functions the MDBs should perform, the Task Force examined a number of "how to" issues, especially in areas where there seemed to be problems that impacted on the ability of the MDBs to perform needed functions successfully.

It should be noted that a number of Task Force members have had experience with both successful and unsuccessful MDB programs, and this section is not intended to imply that current MDB operations do not produce successful results in some cases.

However, Task Force members, with their extensive collective firsthand knowledge of MDB programs, also have concerns about a number of aspects of bank operations. These concerns seem to be borne out by the relatively few available rigorous and systematic studies of results of MDB operations in key areas. (The problem of getting good data on the results of MDB programs is discussed further in Recommendation 15, and that of the availability of MDB data to the public is discussed in Recommendation 14.)

One of the areas of concern is the problems the MDBs have had in institutional development or in increasing the ability of a country to use its human, organizational, and financial resources. Improving the functioning of developing-country institutions is fundamental to almost all aspects of development, from macroeconomic management and operation and maintenance of infrastructure to enforcement of environmental regulations and management of social programs. Numerous studies, as well as the views of Task Force members and speakers, indicate that this is an area of serious MDB weakness.

At a December 19, 1996, World Bank seminar, one of the speakers noted that recently tallied Bank information (from the Operations Evaluation Department) showed that only 19 percent of the Bank's Technical Assistance projects looked at in 1995 were rated as performing satisfactorily.[13] The World Bank summary of evaluation results published in 1996 reported that: "Institutional development goals were substantially achieved in 39 percent of operations—better than the 30 percent in the 1993 cohort [group studied] and the average of 31 percent for the last five years, but again a low figure."[14]

A separate World Bank report on "Two Decades of Lending for Urban Development" gave virtually identical results, noting, "Though a goal of two-thirds of completed projects, institutional development was substantially achieved in only 32 percent of completed projects (slightly higher than the Bank average)."[15] A 1996 World Bank evaluation found that among recently completed projects for electric power in Africa "only 27 percent substantially achieved their institutional development goals."[16]

Another major problem area for MDB projects is whether they lead to results that are sustained after external funding ceases. (Unlike a number of UN agencies and bilateral donor programs that give, on a grant basis, food and other aid that is meant to be directly consumed to meet an immediate humanitarian need, MDB programs are meant to be investments that will lead to future improvements in productivity and living standards.) Again, the World Bank's Operations Evaluation Department presents a less than optimal prognosis:

> Forty-four percent of the operations [evaluated in 1995] are expected to sustain their benefits throughout the operational phase which follows the completion of loan disbursements. This proportion is little different from last year's evaluation cohort and the average for 1989–94. But the proportion of operations judged unlikely to sustain their benefits dropped to 20 percent from 24 percent in 1993.... In Africa 23 percent of operations were rated likely to be sustainable. On the other hand, only 26 percent, down from 31 percent in 1989–94, were rated as unlikely to be sustainable.[17]

13. Statement by Gary McMahon, consultant to the World Bank, Seminar of the World Bank Research Department, Washington, D.C., December 19, 1996.

14. World Bank, OED, *World Bank 1994 Evaluation Results* (Washington, D.C.: World Bank, 1996), 1.

15. World Bank, OED, "Two Decades of Lending for Urban Development," *OED Précis* (Washington, D.C.: World Bank, December 1994), 3.

16. World Bank, OED, "Bank Lending for Electric Power in Africa: Time for a Reappraisal," *OED Précis* (Washington, D.C.: World Bank, January 1996), 1.

A recent U.S. General Accounting Office report (that only looked at the World Bank) decided after analyzing much Bank internal data that the World Bank seemed to have about a 70 percent success rate (defined as projects that "substantially achieved objectives") in meeting physical objectives such as constructing buildings, while its success in achieving other objectives such as institutional development, financial reform, and macroeconomic and sector policy reform was around 30–35 percent.[18] Again, the World Bank's summary of 1994 evaluation results seemed to come to a similar conclusion when it noted about projects in the important agriculture sector, "Many managed to meet their physical goals for installing new facilities but were ultimately judged unsatisfactory and/or unlikely to maintain their benefits."[19]

Note: Almost all of the specific data pertained to the World Bank, but Task Force members were not optimistic that evaluation data for the regional banks, had credible comparable material been available, would have shown improved results in these areas, and there was concern that some of the regional banks' results could be worse. The EBRD's projects are too new to be judged on a comparable basis.

The Task Force was concerned that the MDBs appear to be having difficulty with the "nonphysical construction" aspects of their mandate—the very things for which the growing private-sector flows are least likely to take over their burden. Therefore, the Task Force thought it critical that the MDBs address what appear to be the weaknesses in their operating systems and modalities that result in these problems.

For the World Bank, President Wolfensohn's Strategic Compact, approved by the Bank's Executive Board on March 31, 1997, acknowledges some of the problems discussed in the following sections. From the brief descriptions provided by the Compact of proposed changes it was not possible to know if they appear likely to resolve these problems.

MDB OPERATIONS: The Problem of Scale and Flexibility

Background

The MDBs are entities accustomed to operating on a large scale. For several of them, loans of $500 million are not uncommon. (The average loan size for the World Bank is $80 million.) In some circumstances this capability is good; it gives the MDBs a capacity nearly unique among public development entities to deal with large-scale problems.

The MDBs' focus on large-scale lending flows from their traditional role in transferring resources and is based on the belief that a binding constraint on growth

---

17. World Bank, OED, *World Bank 1994 Evaluation Results* (Washington, D.C.: World Bank, 1996), 1.

18. U.S. General Accounting Office (GAO) Report, *World Bank: U.S. Interests Supported, but Oversight Needed to Help Ensure Improved Performance* (Washington, D.C.: GAO, September 1996), 42–43.

19. World Bank, OED, *World Bank 1994 Evaluation Results* (Washington, D.C.: World Bank, 1996), 32.

and development for many countries is a lack of financial resources. On the basis of accumulated experience, however, it is now considered far less clear that transferring sizable resources will lead to growth or development or that public-sector resource transfers are needed in some countries and sectors.

Importance of small projects. Meanwhile, many observers believe that the MDBs' operating systems remain too geared to lending on a large scale without the flexibility to devote high-priority, high-quality attention to programs that are not related to large-scale lending. Some of the most important contributions the MDBs can make are not linked to the provision of large loans, but often require considerable expenditure of MDB staff time and expertise as well as leadership in areas such as

- [ ] institutional development for all kinds of institutions, from maintaining infrastructure to safeguarding the soundness of the banking system to upgrading the enforcement of environmental policies;

- [ ] experimental or pilot projects, to devise means to deal with difficult problems;

- [ ] other types of high-priority technical assistance such as the development of regulatory frameworks (these activities can have a greater impact than large loans, but they can lose needed flexibility and perceived priority if grouped into larger projects);

- [ ] microenterprise development, support for environmentally beneficial small enterprises, addressing gaps in agricultural input and marketing services, and other areas where MDB leadership in removing policy obstacles and bringing together disparate parties is needed, but large-scale lending is not;

- [ ] energy conservation, nontraditional sources of energy, and other areas where the most desirable technical solutions may argue for a small project;

- [ ] work in the smallest and poorest countries, which do not have the absorptive or debt-service capacity to use large loans; and

- [ ] work in the richer developing countries, which are nearing graduation and do not need resource transfers but can benefit from MDB expertise.

Importance of staff-intensive projects. Another problem for the banks is the increasing recognition of the importance of staff-intensive activities. Institutional development, when done sensitively and thoroughly, is highly staff-intensive, as is the provision of policy advice that is well tailored to local needs, perceptions, and problems. In addition, if the need to consult with project beneficiaries is taken seriously, it is likely to make very large-scale projects of some types difficult and mandate a more time-consuming and probably more expensive process of project preparation and implementation. (Discussed in Recommendation 11a.)

Need for flexibility in MDB processes and changes in the incentive structure. In spite of the general recognition of the problem of scale or excessive focus on "moving money" since the World Bank published its *Report of the Portfolio Management Task Force* (Wapenhans Report) in 1992, and the three older regional banks followed with similar reviews, little seems to have been done on a bank-wide, systematic basis either to establish more flexible procedures that make doing small, inexpensive projects easier or to remove disincentives for ambitious staff to devote attention to activities that are not related to or will not quickly lead to a large loan.

A January 1996 report by the World Bank Human Capital Department describes the problem in the most specific way:

> The current rules governing what can and cannot be done in Bank projects have grown out of ideas developed in earlier decades reaching back to the 1950s, when large physical infrastructure projects like dams and roads were the norm. Although extensive changes have been made to accommodate new sectors such as education and health, staff in the social sectors often still feel they face an uphill battle in getting their problems and requirements adequately understood and appreciated. For example, it can be a struggle to get approval to depart from the traditional blueprinting approach to project design in order to take a more process-oriented approach.... Another example is that pilot-testing of new project ideas—a sensible step before going to large-scale is often impeded by unnecessarily difficult hurdles to obtaining approval and support.... If piloting is to be supported and encouraged—with the full support and commitment of the Bank then greater attention needs to be given to making it easier and faster to do pilots.... This means that not only the requirements but also the Bank culture's attitudes toward small loans need to change to be much more favorable to and supportive of innovative testing of promising new project approaches.[20]

A follow-up to the Inter-American Development Bank's internal portfolio review reaches a similar conclusion:

> Experience with implementing social loans suggests that greater flexibility in the duration of loans, earlier disbursements for preparing human resources, and creating some pilot experiments would strengthen project performance.[21]

One of the large international NGOs that works extensively with the banks at the project level wrote in 1995 about the World Bank,

> Unfortunately, the development of genuinely participative structures is hard to reconcile with the Bank's top-down approach to development, which remains firmly in place. Staff are still constrained by inflexible procedures governing procurement and disbursement. They are still based mainly in Washington, and

---

20. World Bank, "Getting Results in the Social Sectors," *Report of the Human Capital Department* (Washington, D.C.: World Bank, January 16, 1996), 8, 11, 21–22.

21. Inter-American Development Bank, *1995 Report on Improving Portfolio Management* (Washington, D.C.: IDB, June 1996), 26.

rarely develop a rapport with local organizations; they are unable to monitor effectively the performance of implementing agencies; and there are few real incentives for staff to carry out participatory work, given pressure to achieve lending targets. In short, the World Bank's practice is likely to continue falling short of its aspirations to become a listening bank.[22]

Need for flexibility in other operational aspects. The need for greater flexibility came up regarding several other areas. One was the need to adapt procurement procedures to new situations, including new developments in environmental and information technology. Without compromising standards of open international competition, the MDBs should be more flexible in adapting their procurement requirements to the realities of current commercial practice and the needs of specific projects, including being open to the possibility of a competitively selected single vendor being eligible to perform preproposal engineering and consulting studies as well as to implement the resulting proposal (e.g., new procurement situations presented by Build-Operate-Transfer [BOT] projects and in the fast-changing field of information technology). The World Bank already has made some changes to allow more flexible procurement in the case of social development and social fund projects.

Change Needed

In order to deal successfully with what most observers consider to be the ingrained MDB focus on "moving money," the institutions need to develop new basic processes for selecting projects, rating the importance of incoming information, and allocating resources internally to reflect sustainable development priorities other than large-scale lending. They also need to change the complex web of formal and informal incentives by which the organizations signal existing staff and new recruits about the qualities and achievements for which they will be rewarded.

Commensurately, shareholders need to recognize that measures of administrative costs per dollar lent will be adversely affected by these changes. However, the validity of such measures as an indication of MDB performance in current circumstances is doubtful.

In most of the MDBs, there are cases where the prevailing system has been changed as a means of partly remedying problems. Usually these actions have been due to interested and inventive staff or have occurred in small, atypical programs that are often extensively publicized. These instances usually cover only a small fraction of bank activities, however, and operating systems attuned to traditional objectives have not been changed yet to assure or even facilitate these outcomes. As one of the papers prepared for the Task Force noted, "The problem is that the new policy intentions [of some banks] and directives are being promulgated within an organization whose operating systems are all designed to transfer capital and exploit technical skills."[23] The challenge now is to adopt new systems and

---

22. Oxfam, Policy Department, *A Case for Reform: Fifty Years of the IMF and World Bank* (Oxford: Oxfam, 1995), 36–37.

incentives that are comprehensive and coherent and that motivate the majority of staff to focus appropriate attention on goals not related to loan quantity.

> **RECOMMENDATION 9. MDB Operations: The Problems of Scale and Flexibility—Need for More Flexible Processes and Incentives.** The MDBs should change and make more flexible the elements of their core processes and operating modalities that currently combine to place institutional priority on large-scale lending. New processes and incentives need to be put in place that encourage capable and ambitious staff to place priority on activities and projects that will not quickly lead to the approval of new large loans, when this alternative focus is warranted by country needs. These more flexible processes and incentives need to be available and supported across the full range of an institution's operations, not just in small special programs.

> **BENCHMARK.** *Each MDB has adopted and made public clear measures both in (1) core processes and (2) staff incentives that encourage and facilitate priority attention to nonlending activities (e.g., leadership in support of microenterprise), small or pilot projects (including institutional development), and staff-intensive work in project preparation and implementation in such areas as beneficiary analysis and participation.*

MDB OPERATIONS: The Problem of Accountability

Background

One of the problems that has plagued MDB projects is the issue of what entity is responsible if bank projects fail, especially if the failure is due to a lack of adequate implementation after the loan is approved by the MDB's board of executive directors. A widely disseminated 1994 World Bank publication says, "Operations supported by Bank lending are primarily the responsibility of borrowers."[24] This and similar statements that have been made by many MDB officials over the years create confusion about what entity is accountable to MDB donors when projects do not produce intended results due to implementation problems. MDB statements on this issue differ considerably, with most banks acknowledging a fiduciary responsibility, but how this is interpreted differs, especially regarding project implementation.

Because borrowers are obligated to repay all MDB loans, clearly borrowing entities are responsible to their own citizens (if they are governments) or their shareholders (if they are private corporations) for good stewardship of the resources that must be repaid. In addition, however, all MDB funds lent to

---

23. Paul J. Nelson, "The Multilateral Development Banks and Rapid Sustained Poverty Reduction: Progress, Limitations, and Recommendations" (paper prepared for the CSIS Task Force on the United States and the MDBs, Washington, D.C., 1996), 15.

24. World Bank, *Assessing Development Effectiveness* (Washington, D.C.: World Bank, May 1994), 1.

borrowers either are contributions (in the case of concessional windows) or are available because taxpayers in donor countries are guaranteeing their repayment (in the case of nonconcessional windows). They are made available for the purpose of achieving economic-development and poverty-reduction objectives and are not justified solely as sound investments that will be repaid. Therefore, in the Task Force's view, the MDBs should be held accountable by their shareholders for the results of their projects.

Obviously, there are a number of ways in which the MDBs can seek to fulfill this responsibility. They can actively help borrowers to understand and fulfill their obligations or they can maintain a more "hands-off" approach. Which MDB role is the most useful probably depends on the country and activity involved.

Change Needed

Whatever style the MDB may choose in a particular case, the Task Force believes it should be clearly understood that shareholders hold the MDB responsible for the results of the projects they fund. If the borrower is not fulfilling its responsibilities for critical aspects of the project, it is the bank's responsibility to know this, help correct the problem, or stop disbursement on the project. In looking at future projects, if there is not good reason to believe the obstacles to the borrower's adequate performance in meeting its obligations (with whatever help the MDB believes it appropriate to provide) have been removed, the MDB should not go forward with the loan.

A system where the MDB claims it is not responsible for the results of a project because the borrower failed to honor its obligations, but with the MDB continuing to make disbursements on that loan and approving others to the same borrower, is unacceptable.

> **RECOMMENDATION 10. MDB Operations: The Problem of Accountability.** The MDBs should be considered accountable to their shareholders for the results of their projects. If the borrower is not implementing the project adequately or meeting other obligations important for project success, the MDB needs to help correct the problem or stop funding the project.
>
> **BENCHMARK.** *Each MDB has accepted this responsibility.*

MDB OPERATIONS: The Problem of Location

Background

A significant part of MDB efforts is directed at improving the productivity and expanding the choices of people living in poor urban areas and rural villages. The Task Force thinks that how MDB programs affect the lives of individuals is of key importance. This does not mean that the MDBs should be physically present in all these areas, but it does mean that the links by which the MDBs ascertain the needs of those who will be affected by projects and ensure that their projects respond effectively to these needs should be clear and well functioning.

The MDBs are increasingly funding activities that directly affect the lives of large numbers of often-vulnerable people. The growing programs of the MDBs in areas such as land titling, natural resources management, urban development, improving the quality of education, health, family planning, and social safety net programs, and many types of agricultural activities impact local people directly. These activities also depend for their success on local people supporting them, using their services, and helping to sustain them after external funding has stopped. Therefore, it is now even more important for the success of MDB programs that the link between the MDB and the village be clear and functioning well. (Although concerns about local linkages may be most severe in these kinds of projects, they are also important for almost all programs aimed at developing and implementing regulatory structures or improving institutions.)

Often in the past the MDBs simply assumed that borrowing governments would supply what linkages were needed to local people. Where developing-country governments can and will see that these linkages work, this is the optimal situation. For projects to go forward successfully in countries where the government does not have the capability or the will to maintain these linkages, however, the MDB needs to work with the borrowing government to forge or strengthen the linkages.

Developing strong enough linkages to the right local groups for projects to be successful is not easy. These programs usually must function in dispersed locations and may involve the participation of national, provincial, and local government officials as well as the individuals who are supposed to benefit. Often the poor beneficiaries are in a relatively unequal position in their own community, and may be ethnically and culturally distinct from those controlling the central government. In such situations, even if a borrower's senior national leadership is committed to a program, assuring that those who run it at the provincial and local level are competent, honest, and working in the beneficiaries' interest is not easy.

Identifying projects that respond to local needs. The first challenge faced by the MDB is knowing precisely what are the binding constraints in a particular area. It is not always obvious what mix of economic, ecological, political, or social constraints are leading to ecological damage, land ownership problems, or poor-quality education in local schools. Many times knowing the causes of the problems requires substantial local knowledge, and developing proposed solutions requires more than technical expertise.

It is difficult under current MDB operating modalities to develop this depth of local expertise. As former World Bank official Barend de Vries has noted,

> To be effective in assisting countries…Bank staff must have intimate knowledge of these countries' culture, institutions, politics, and social fabric, as well as the economic and technical ramifications of an anti-poverty program. Staff stationed in resident offices will need to be strengthened and work closely with NGO workers. At present, the [World] Bank's poverty assessments are technically competent reports, but they are highly standardized and make little

allowance for countries' cultural and social characteristics. This must change if the Bank is to put flesh on its skeleton models....[25]

Several speakers at a recent World Bank seminar indicated that some MDB failures in institutional development may stem from misdiagnosing the problem due to unfamiliarity with local conditions. Often institutional failings may be attributed to a lack of knowledge of what to do or how to do it, when the real problem is a political one.[26]

In formulating projects that will have an impact on local people, it is very important that whoever is identifying and designing the project have in-depth dialogue with the whole gamut of local groups that will affect its success. It is essential that the results of these dialogues be recognized as important and not get "lost in the shuffle" as senior MDB managers make decisions about projects.

Achieving a solid meeting of the minds with the local groups needed to make a project a success is likely to require significant and time-consuming project preparatory work. A few visits by a consultant or a meeting or two with several local representatives selected by the government probably will not be enough to lay the groundwork for a project that will have a major impact on local life or on power relationships in the village.

For this kind of project, the MDBs' current project-development arrangements, based on short visits by headquarters-based staff, supplemented by consultants' reports, all of which generally must fit within well-defined project preparation schedules and guidelines, often seem inadequate. Daniel Bradlow and Claudio Grossman wrote in 1996, "[The Bretton Woods institutions'] present bureaucratic structures are not well suited to planning and executing operations that emphasize public participation and the free flow of information. These operations require structures that can encourage and respond to actions initiated from the broad base of stakeholders in the operations rather than structures that rely on actions being initiated from the senior levels of their own and their borrowers' institutions."[27] David Hunter of the Center for International Environmental Law wrote in 1996, "Even where [World] Bank staff adopt participatory methods, the quality of the participation is often quite low. Many borrowing country NGOs leave consultations or participatory processes feeling that their participation was irrelevant."[28]

A study prepared for the Danish aid agency (Danida) and based on fieldwork in four countries came to the same conclusion regarding specifically both the World Bank and the African Development Bank:

---

25. Barend A. de Vries, "The World Bank's Focus on Poverty," in *The World Bank: Lending on a Global Scale; Rethinking Bretton Woods*, vol. III, eds. Jo Marie Griesgraber and Bernhard G. Gunter (London: Pluto Press in association with the Center for Concern, 1996), 76.

26. Discussion at the World Bank Research Department Seminar, Washington, D.C., December 19, 1996.

27. Daniel D. Bradlow and Claudio Grossman, "Adjusting the Bretton Woods Institutions to Contemporary Realities" in *Development: New Paradigms and Principles for the Twenty-First Century; Rethinking Bretton Woods*, vol. II, eds. Jo Marie Griesgraber and Bernhard G. Gunter (London: Pluto Press in association with the Center for Concern, 1996), 37–38.

28. David Hunter, *The Role of the World Bank in Strengthening Governance, Civil Society, and Human Rights* (Washington, D.C.: Center for International Environmental Law, January 1996), 11.

The [World] Bank's relative weaknesses concern its presence at country level which is insufficient to fully utilize its analytical capacity and its diverse development instruments. There is a gap between the centralized organization of the bank and its increasing involvement in institutionally and politically complex operations in the hearts of the politico-administrative setup in developing countries.

AfDB's mode of operation at country level is first and foremost characterized by insufficient presence...it can be said that the few case studies confirmed the overall picture of an agency being too far away, both physically and technically, from actual operations to be able to ensure proper quality of design and effective implementation.[29]

Monitoring project implementation, fixing problems, and checking who gets benefits. If the distance between project sites and those in MDBs making decisions about the projects is a problem in designing activities, it is a more difficult problem in checking to see if the activity is going well.

When the MDBs' major function was to construct infrastructure, they could usually track project implementation by receiving periodic reports from a respected engineering firm on physical progress and expenditures. The MDBs have continued to use more or less this system to try to supervise progress on much more complex and hard-to-measure undertakings. In these situations, local elites may have strong incentives to divert benefits and central governments face temptations to overlook problems to keep funds flowing. The MDBs rely largely on written reports from borrowing governments (or consultants hired by these governments) about whether projects are on track. Consultants selected by a government for this work can vary greatly in qualifications, ties to affected parties, and stake in a particular outcome. Direct MDB oversight is provided by short-term visiting missions or the small in-country MDB staff, if there is one.

There has been substantial concern for the last several years about the adequacy of MDB project implementation. The need for MDBs to devote more attention to implementing ongoing projects, compared with designing new ones, was a key finding of the portfolio reviews of the World Bank, the IDB, the ADB, and the AfDB.[30] Although the banks have put out proclamations that they will improve project supervision and implementation and some steps have been taken, little evidence was found of the kind of far-reaching and comprehensive reforms that appear needed, or of improved results.

The World Bank report published in 1996 on the results of the most recent evaluations notes:

---

29. Danida, Danish Ministry of Foreign Affairs, *Effectiveness of Multilateral Agencies at Country Level* (Denmark: Danida, 1991), 2.31–32, 2.34.

30. The portfolio reviews are the World Bank's *Report of the Portfolio Management Task Force* (Wapenhans Report) (Washington, D.C.: World Bank, 1992); *Report to the Task Force on Improving Project Quality in the Asian Development Bank* (Schultz Report) (Manila: ADB, 1994); *Managing Effective Development in the Inter-American Development Bank* (Tapoma Report) (Washington, D.C.: IDB, 1993); *The Quest for Quality in the African Development Bank* (Knox Report) (Abidjan: AfDB, 1994).

Yet much current supervision work still gives short shrift to those factors that would allow the Bank to advise mid-course corrections where needed to achieve projects' development objectives…. Further evidence that this needs to be addressed by the Bank with some urgency comes from a recent OED review of Bank monitoring and evaluation practices in approved operations. The study, based on a review of 164 investment projects, recognizes that significant progress is being made at the working level, but concludes that monitoring and evaluation is still a neglected feature of quality assurance—thus confirming the views of borrowers and staff referred to earlier in this chapter.[31]

A former U.S. executive director at the World Bank, E. Patrick Coady, painted a similar picture in his November 1993 report following a field visit to Madagascar:

> At the end of it all, there seems to be a basic disconnect between the World Bank and field implementation. The reasons are understandable, explainable, but the fact is that progress is disappointing. There is no question in my mind that the time-honored mechanisms for implementation, supervision, monitoring, and coordination have to be reformed and restructured.[32]

The Danida study was more specific about the problem:

> The development banks [referring to the World Bank, ADB, and AfDB] are generally too far away from the social structures of implementation to be able to guarantee that project benefits reach the marginalized target groups rather than the local elites…. The combination of the Bank's separation from implementation, its specialist supervision system, the capital intensity of its operations, and in general its centralized organization provides it with comparative disadvantages in implementation support of projects that are either socially or institutionally complex…. Similarly the [World] Bank's non-involvement during project implementation prevents it from offering sufficient support and control on socially complex projects to ensure that, for example, particular target groups are reached in spite of the interests of local elites.[33]

More recently, a June 28, 1996, World Bank OED study on the effectiveness of environmental assessments found:

> One of the weakest aspects of the Bank's use of Environmental Assessment policies and guidelines during project implementation has been related to lax supervision of environmental concerns during project implementation…. Several of the Bank's Regional Vice Presidents commented that while it is true that environmental components could do with more supervision, that is also the case for most project components (including procurement, project accounts, audits, etc.).[34]

---

31. World Bank, OED, *1994 Evaluation Results* (Washington, D.C.: World Bank, 1996), 6, 84.

32. E. Patrick Coady, *Catalyzing Changes in Conserving Biodiversity in the Field: Madagascar—Case Study I* (Washington, D.C.: Conservation International, November 1993), 5.

33. Danida, Danish Ministry of Foreign Affairs, *Effectiveness of Multilateral Agencies at Country Level* (Denmark: Danida, 1991), 38, 2.29, 2.32.

A July 1996 IDB report concludes:

The dearth of Bank Staff in Country offices with sufficient technical experience and sector knowledge in such areas as environment, health, education, and modernization of the State, is a constraint which impedes needed flexibility in execution and reprogramming where conditions have changed at the country level.[35]

Finally, the 1996 World Bank OED study on "Bank Lending for Electric Power in Africa" found that "Bank staff are often too remote or lack the skills to supervise technical assistance."[36]

Current MDB efforts to monitor the local situation. The MDBs' distant approach to project monitoring and supervision stems from the decisions they made decades ago to be primarily headquarters-based institutions. The World Bank, which has a total international professional staff of about 6,000, permanently assigns about 300 of them to its field offices (not all of which are in borrowing countries).[37]

In the face of their lack of local staff, the MDBs have turned to various alternatives when borrowing-government implementation is weak, some of which have also failed to solve the problem. The Danida study lays out the shortcomings of excessive reliance on consultants: "The problem is that both long- and short-term consultants require strong support and supervision from Bank staff."[38]

A more recent alternative tried by some banks has been to work directly with local governments, in the hope that they will be more responsive to local needs. Although this may prove helpful in some cases, several observers express doubts that this will be an effective response across the board to the problem of flawed linkages between MDBs and local project beneficiaries. Oxfam expressed the following concern:

For example, in Brazil the [World] Bank has seen "municipalisation" as a mechanism for addressing problems associated with its projects.... In the Planafloro project case, the World Bank has proposed transferring administrative responsibility from a State government, notorious for allegations of

---

34. World Bank, OED, *Effectiveness of Environmental Assessments and National Environmental Action Plans* (Washington, D.C.: World Bank, June 28, 1996), 30–31.

35. Inter-American Development Bank, *Report on the Action Plan for Meeting the Needs of the C & D Countries* (Washington, D.C.: IDB, July 1996), 11.

36. World Bank, OED, "Bank Lending for Electric Power in Africa: Time for a Reappraisal," *OED Précis* (Washington, D.C.: World Bank, January 1996), 3.

37. This is supplemented by 120 professional-level consultants and 550 local professional staff, who do professional work but whose relationship to local entities is necessarily different. The ADB has about the same percentage of its professional staff assigned to field offices in borrowing countries (40 out of 664), as does the EBRD (33 out of 549), while the IDB has a slightly larger share (160 out of 1763). The AfDB abolished all its field offices a few years ago, but is in the process of reestablishing some field posts. Source: Data supplied to the Task Force by various MDBs in the fall of 1996.

38. Danida, Danish Ministry of Foreign Affairs, *Effectiveness of Multilateral Agencies at Country Level* (Denmark: Danida, 1991), 2.30.

corruption and protection of vested interests, to municipal bodies. The problem is that municipal bodies in the project area share many of the problems associated with State bodies. Similar problems have emerged with the Small Farmers Support Project in north-east Brazil.[39]

Change Needed

The MDBs need to make more effective efforts to make the linkages between themselves and their beneficiaries (especially poor ones) work well. In countries with the commitment and competence to maintain adequate links to local beneficiaries, the banks need to do nothing different. Everything that can be left to the borrowers' responsibility should be. In the larger group of countries where the commitment or capacity is inconsistent or unreliable, the MDBs need to be more proactive in monitoring and knowing what is going on with their projects, working to fix problems before projects fail, and checking to see if benefits are going to those who need them.

The first thing the MDBs must do is make it clear to borrowing countries that they are serious about taking the beneficiaries' views into account. This means turning the hortatory statements the banks make about the need for local participation in projects into concrete plans to assure that it happens.

Making local participation a reality. Listening to the views of the people who will be affected by a project and having a meaningful dialogue with them over whether and how a project will help them, followed by continued dialogue as implementation proceeds, will be a major change in how MDB projects are managed. It will require significant changes in how much and what kind of interaction project designers and implementers have with "the people who live there."

> **RECOMMENDATION 11a. MDB Operations: The Problem of Location—Assuring Local Participation.** All of the MDBs need to
>
> - develop a screening process to decide which possible project activities require what kind of participation by which local groups (as with most material on upcoming projects, this should be public; see Recommendation 14);
>
> - establish a project preparation and implementation cycle that readily accommodates the activities needed to generate the depth of local dialogue required (this includes the availability of staffing and other resources required for this work); and
>
> - put in place a system to monitor whether the planned local participation is taking place, keep an eye on the quality of the dialogue and its results, and develop plans to deal with problems encountered.

---

39. Oxfam, Policy Department, *A Case for Reform: Fifty Years of the IMF and World Bank* (Oxford: Oxfam, 1995), 36.

> **BENCHMARK.** *Each MDB has in place a credible system to achieve these objectives.*

Assuring better MDB knowledge of what is happening during project implementation. The banks need to do a better job of knowing what is going on during project implementation and, when project success is threatened, working with borrowers proactively to solve problems. If it appears that problems cannot be fixed or the MDB and borrowers cannot agree on a course of action, the project should be canceled.

There are a number of ways by which the MDBs can do this. The simplest is to pursue implementation issues with more energy and zeal using current methods. A 1993 World Bank Financial Report and Auditing Task Force reported that "Financial statements [on projects being implemented] when received are frequently not reviewed and if so, are reviewed by staff without the necessary skills to adequately identify significant problems and to recommend and follow up with the appropriate remedial action."[40] A paper prepared for the Task Force by a former World Bank staff member, who explicitly checked on whether previous problems had been remedied, indicated that poor monitoring by bank staff of the financial situation of credit intermediaries had long been a contributing factor in problems with credit projects.[41]

In many cases, however, no matter how good a job staff members do using current methods, the distance between the MDBs and where their projects are supposed to have an impact may preclude their being thoroughly aware of what is happening on the ground. This would particularly pertain to projects where the major impact is hard to ascertain (e.g., improved fairness in the functioning of rural land markets, improved quality of social services) or where the temptations are great for richer groups to divert benefits.

In these cases, the banks need to find new ways to get more reliable information on how projects are proceeding and who is benefiting in time to make midcourse corrections.

One option is to station more MDB staff with project monitoring responsibilities in the field. Although residing in a country's capital is no guarantee that MDB project officers will know what's happening in remote project areas, it is easier for them to get there and more likely that they will fully understand the local context when they make a site visit. It is also likely that they will have better local contacts and sources of information about the interlocking web of relationships and interests that will help determine the actions of all the local players, including the borrowing government and the consultants it may hire.

A recent internal IDB report makes the case:

---

40. World Bank, *Report of the Financial Reporting and Auditing Task Force* (Washington, D.C.: World Bank, October 8, 1993), 3.

41. J. D. Von Pischke, "Risk, Reporting, and Relevance in World Bank Credit Projects" (paper prepared for the CSIS Task Force on the United States and the MDBs, Washington, D.C., August 14, 1996), 2.

Therefore, a key factor in improving portfolio performance is the number and quality of professional staff that the [Inter-American Development] Bank assigns to portfolio management. The number of Country Office staff must be appropriate for the workload, and their skills must reflect the sectoral composition of the workload. As indicated in the Country Office Task Force Report, there is now a gap in the number and skills mix of the sector specialists when compared with the portfolio under management. In the absence of efforts to increase the numbers of specialists and readjust skills, the gap will widen over time.[42]

The value of more in-country staff in supervising social-sector programs was reiterated by Population Action International in its report on "The World Bank's Role in Global Population Efforts: An Agenda for Effective Action":

Many of these implementation problems can be attributed to the lack of adequate in-country supervision. The Bank's operating style is to utilize periodic "missions" or teams of headquarters staff, often accompanied by short-term consultants, who visit a country periodically to design and supervise a project. Because these visits are typically infrequent and composition of these teams often changes from one mission to the next, supervision missions rarely provide continuity, follow-up or most importantly, sustained technical assistance. In the limited time available, these teams are often preoccupied with physical and financial targets. The absence of a strong continuous in-country presence often contributes to implementation delays and problems with complex project components. It is noteworthy that in the few countries where the [World] Bank has appointed resident population advisors, they have helped the programs significantly.[43]

Having more staff stationed in borrowing countries does not mean going overboard and having 200-person MDB missions in borrowing countries that usurp the project implementation role from local authorities. It just means having enough people responsible to the MDB with project-monitoring responsibilities in a position to know what is happening, so that problems can be fixed before project funds are wasted or benefits diverted. This approach also would require assuring that MDB staff in the field have sufficient authority to do their jobs adequately and eliminating duplicative headquarters functions.

As a way to know more about what is going on with their projects, the MDBs could also choose to rely more on other in-country groups. Appendix C summarizes some of the Task Force discussion and papers on the prospects for MDB partnerships with other groups to help solve some of their problems with local linkages. Potential local partners could include private nonprofit organizations, for-profit entities, local or international foundations, local universities or research

---

42. Inter-American Development Bank, *1995-IDB Report on Follow-Up to the Tapoma Portfolio Review* (Washington, D.C.: IDB, 1995), 27.

43. Sharon L. Camp and Shanti R. Conley, *The World Bank's Role in Global Population Efforts: An Agenda for Effective Action* (Washington, D.C.: Population Action International, July 1989), 20.

institutes (perhaps in partnership with developed country counterparts), and other public institutions with complementary capabilities (e.g., the UN Children's Fund [UNICEF] or IFAD [International Fund for Agricultural Development]). Clearly, not all partnerships would provide reliable additional information on the local situation, and the banks would need to check carefully on the extent to which specific types of ties to particular groups are proving effective in remedying on-the-ground implementation problems.

One of the explanations often given for sketchy project monitoring arrangements is the desire by the MDBs to keep their administrative costs down, and it is true that some arrangements for improved monitoring would add to administrative costs (e.g., it costs several hundred thousand dollars in salary and expenses to add an experienced professional to an MDB's field staff). On the other hand, given the size of the MDB loans and the percentage of them that evaluation reports show to be at risk, it seems that adding relatively small amounts to administrative costs to try to get better results from much larger loans is an acceptable trade-off. (MDB administrative costs are usually funded from the institution's net income, and surpluses are often used to fund additional concessional-window lending. If more resources are used for better monitoring, it means that slightly less may be available for new loans.)

RECOMMENDATION 11b. MDB Operations: The Problem of Location—Obtaining Better Knowledge of Implementation Status. The MDBs need to develop better means of checking on project implementation (especially whether programs to serve poor groups are effective and are reaching those intended) and of assuring that changes are made when program objectives are threatened.

BENCHMARK. To demonstrate that it is carefully following project implementation and to facilitate receiving useful input from outside groups and individuals, each MDB prepares and makes public annually in the national language a short report on the status of all projects being implemented in each country.

This report discusses each project separately, listing name, amount of MDB loan and local financial contribution, project objectives, and likelihood of achieving objectives. If there are serious problems with the project, they are described, along with what is being done about them and who is responsible for next steps. This report notes the local participation planned and how this is proceeding. Compilations of these country-status reports are publicly available. (Note: A report similar to this is currently prepared and made public annually by the International Fund for Agricultural Development.)

MDB OPERATIONS: Fixing the Gap between Rhetoric and Reality

Background

If only official policies and public pronouncements were examined, it would be assumed that most of the problems raised in the previous sections had long since been resolved. The MDBs have been promising for years to change their incentive structure, to end the pressure to "move money," to focus more on project implementation, and to "listen to beneficiaries." The evidence the Task Force saw indicated quite clearly, however, that these remained problems for most of the banks. This raised the broader issue of the apparent discrepancy between MDB policies/ public rhetoric and their actions at the operational level.

This problem was described most eloquently in relation to the World Bank by Professor Gustav Ranis of Yale University in his paper for the 1994 Bretton Woods Commission:

> One must acknowledge the existence of two circulatory systems in operation within the Bank. One—encompassing the President's office, the Bank's research wings, and sometimes even the chief economist in each of the regions—is concerned with innovative ideas, with deciding the subject and enhancing the quality of the annual World Development Reports, with focusing on whatever key policy topic or topics may be at the moment…. The other encompasses the operating departments, where the continuous flow of project and program lending approvals is what matters, and where it is generally recognized that the longer-term chances for recognition and promotion are largely tied to quantitative lending performance.
>
> The existence of the two circulatory systems, with relatively little capillary action between them, means that the Bank suffers from a severe case of schizophrenia. When the two objectives come into conflict—and they usually do— the need for maintaining the flow of project approvals invariably overcomes the concern with the quality enhancement of the loan instruments and, more importantly, their overall impact on the borrower country's performance.[44]

At a December 1996 seminar held by the World Bank's Research Department, the problem was put more delicately when a Bank research staffer remarked that there were a lot of points all seminar attendees agreed upon but the "real gap is with the practitioners."

Many examples of this problem have come to the Task Force's attention. The problem seemed to be particularly acute in the area of environment, where, for example, reviews of compliance with the World Bank's resettlement, energy, and integrated pest-management policies have revealed surprisingly little progress toward stated goals. Information on examples that were brought to the Task Force's attention in a detailed way is noted in Appendix D.

---

44. Gustav Ranis, "Defining the Mission of the World Bank Group," in *Bretton Woods: Looking to the Future*, Background Papers for the Bretton Woods Commission (Washington, D.C.: Bretton Woods Commission, July 1994), 76.

Part of the problem seems to be caused by the attempts of the banks to satisfy shareholders that have conflicting views and even at times to satisfy different influential voices in the same shareholder (e.g., the U.S. executive branch and Congress, or different factions in each). As a result, sometimes part of an MDB responds to one influence, and the other part responds to a conflicting influence, or the institution's policy statements and rhetoric go in one direction while its operational activities go in a different direction. One U.S. NGO defines the phenomenon in the World Bank as the "core" doing one thing and the "periphery" another.

In addition to the problem of trying to satisfy multiple masters, the difference between rhetoric and reality in the institutions may also be due to the well-entrenched and powerful bureaucracies that hold sway in most of the banks, compared with changing and sometimes weak senior leadership. Even if senior management wants and intends to deliver on its promises, it may not know how to pull the right bureaucratic levers to do so.

Change Needed

Although this problem exists in many large organizations, it appears that this trait now has gone too far in the MDBs for them to be able to continue to maintain the trust of important U.S. constituencies. It is preferable for the MDBs to point out honestly where they are not capable or do not believe they should change their practices to suit shareholder preferences. If they have made commitments they do not think they can keep or where shareholder positions result in inevitable conflicts, these should be highlighted and alternatives debated. Then, when decisions are made, they should be followed—by the entire institution.

This does not mean that the United States is likely to support an institution that does not have adequate policies in key areas, such as the environment, or that the United States should accept weakened policies. If the way policies are implemented is proving unexpectedly burdensome, however, the United States should be willing to discuss openly the problem and options for solving it, so long as the MDB provides full information (including to concerned public groups) and abides by its governing bodies' decisions once they are made.

> **RECOMMENDATION 12. MDB Operations: Fixing the Gap between Rhetoric and Reality.** Each MDB should take effective steps to ensure that all parts of the institution follow established policies and that major discrepancies between institutional pronouncements and operational practice are curtailed. Where impractical policy commitments have been made or when policies are in conflict, this problem should be discussed and alternatives debated. When there is public interest in a topic, the public should be fully informed about the debate (see Recommendation 14).

> **BENCHMARK.** *There is an absence of instances where an MDB's operations contravene its policies or its practice diverges substantially from its public pronouncements. In cases where this has been a serious problem (e.g., in connection with various environmental policies in the World Bank), the problem has been resolved.*

MDB OPERATIONS: Incentives—Changing the Internal Signals

Background

This report has many references to the need to change the incentive structure within the MDBs. This issue has arisen in connection with ending incentives to lend when country policies are severely flawed or for projects where private funds are available; creating incentives to give priority to important small projects or nonlending initiatives; and strengthening incentives to follow policies on qualitative aspects of projects and on project implementation.

Almost all the MDBs have produced rhetoric along the same lines, although results appear to have been inconsistent or not visible. Changing incentives in such large institutions with entrenched power structures and organizational cultures is not easy. Nevertheless, if the institutional bias in favor of large new lending and against small projects, implementing ongoing projects, and qualitative improvements is not changed, it is unlikely that these institutions can make the reforms needed to receive continuing funding priority.

One of the problems with changing incentives may be that the MDBs developed ways both formal and informal to reward individuals and organizational units for producing new loans on schedule. For such items as qualitative improvement and project implementation, however, the MDBs apparently have not adopted measures to ascertain individual or organizational unit success and link it to personal or unit rewards.

The developmental results of MDB projects have not been linked to individuals or organizational units due to real difficulty in ascertaining results, difficulty in making judgments about the role of exogenous factors that could not have been foreseen, concern about discouraging needed risk taking, and, above all, the problem posed by constant staff rotation.

This incentive structure has led to a situation where only the staff most committed to individual small activities or qualitative aspects (e.g., local relationships, environment, social issues) have made much time for these activities, and in doing so may have left themselves or their units vulnerable to criticism on the new-loan-volume issue.

The lack of MDB systems to hold individuals at any level accountable for program results also has combined with the emphasis within the MDBs on maintaining good interpersonal relationships to make staff reluctant to raise tough questions about proposed projects or to make difficult decisions to terminate projects or to stop lending in the face of poor borrower performance.

Change Needed

Senior managements in the MDBs need to make it clear that results in terms of poverty reduction, economic growth, and environmental sustainability are the institutional priorities, not approval of large loans. In addition to enunciating this, which most have already done, they need to lead an in-depth examination to ferret out the ways in which individuals and organizational units are rewarded with promotions, honors, or increased resources or, conversely, punished within their organization. All of these systems, both official and unofficial, need to be changed in order for a large organization to change the signals it sends to staff.

Also, senior management needs to make it clear that it has the will and capacity to enforce the changed incentives on a sustained basis. This may mean leadership or organizational changes, resolution of precedent-setting cases, continued managerial attention, and so forth.

In addition to these measures, however, MDB leaders need to find specific ways to link performance in areas other than loan volume to organizational units and to individuals, at least at the managerial level. Although frequent rotations and the need to gain experience may argue for not focusing on individual accountability for project results at lower professional levels, it should be possible to devise a system where the results of specific organizational units are tracked and their managers judged upon them.

Obviously, such systems cannot be mechanistic and would require judgments about whether projects selected appeared to be reasonable in light of country conditions when approved, whether adequate efforts were made to resolve implementation problems, and whether sensible judgments were made to continue or halt problem projects. It should not be impossible, however, to devise a system that makes distinctions between reasonable and unreasonable risks and between unforeseeable natural disasters or government changes and the relatively predictable poor performance of long-troubled executing agencies. If this kind of accountability is established for managers of major organizational units, they will have strong incentives to place performance toward achieving the institution's objectives at the center of their official and unofficial rewards system for their own staff.

RECOMMENDATION 13. MDB Operations: Incentives— Changing the Internal Signals.

- The leadership of each MDB should review comprehensively all of the systems by which individuals and organizational units are rewarded with promotions, honors, more desirable assignments, or increased resources to ensure that these systems are signaling management priority on success toward poverty reduction, economic growth, and environmental stewardship— not achieving a large loan volume. These new incentives should continuously be reinforced.

- Each MDB should devise a system by which operational units and their managements are rated by the results of their projects and the quality of the judgments demonstrated toward achieving substantive objectives. Managers should not be judged adversely for working on poorly performing countries, but they reasonably can be held accountable for the decisions they make about how to respond to problems.

BENCHMARK. Each MDB has conducted such a review and made needed changes in its incentive structure. Each bank is implementing a system that looks at the substantive performance of projects

*in major organizational units and examines the quality of manage-
ment performance in relation to results achieved under the
circumstances.*

MDB OPERATIONS: Transparency

Background

The lack of transparency in MDB operations has become a major problem. In spite
of improvements in recent years (largely at the insistence of the U.S. Congress),
most operational documents of the institutions remain unavailable to the public,
and those that are made available become so only after all decisions about them
have been made.

This practice disadvantages above all the citizens and governments of borrowing countries. The people who live in affected areas, and must repay the debt
incurred, are not able to see detailed plans about any aspects of proposed MDB
projects, except those aspects relating to the environment (environmental impact
assessments must be made available to the public 120 days before projects are
approved due to the "Pelosi Amendment" passed by the U.S. Congress), before
they are locked in by final loan agreements approved by the institutions' boards.
Even executive directors normally have access to detailed project proposals only a
week or two before they must vote on them, a quite short time given the amount of
money and information involved. At later stages in the project process, neither borrowing governments nor their citizens have access to most MDBs' regular reports
on project implementation status.

This policy of secrecy about future plans and the status of ongoing operations
sets an example and sends signals that are at variance with stated MDB objectives
of encouraging more transparent and accountable governance in their borrowers. If
the MDBs themselves are untransparent, it is hard to sell the message that openness
and accountability should be critical aspects of governmental behavior.

Current disclosure policies also seriously undercut the effectiveness of incipi-
ent MDB attempts to include beneficiary participation in the design of new projects
and local participation in formulating country lending strategies. It is hard to know
how serious are plans to elicit local participation if the participating individuals can
never see the resulting document (in the case of all country lending strategies
except those of the ADB) or can only see it after its final approval (as is the case for
project proposals in all MDBs).

For citizens and policymakers in donor countries, however, the MDBs' lack of
transparency poses a different problem. As budgets tighten and hard choices
among programs must be made, it is difficult to evaluate the role and performance
of the MDBs accurately. In view of the historic and continuing discrepancy
between the MDBs' rhetoric and their practice, and the history in some institutions
of major project problems, the MDBs do not enjoy a cushion of public trust in the
United States. The lack of access to operational documents in the face of the great
interest of many groups in the United States in examining these documents fuels
this lack of trust and makes it hard for unbiased observers to know exactly what the

banks are doing, how well they are doing it, or what priority they should receive in terms of U.S. funding.

Change Needed

Documents. The Task Force recognizes that at times parties involved with MDB projects have a legitimate need to keep some information confidential, including proprietary corporate data and information affecting borrower government security. Also, all organizations need to have ways to maintain the confidentiality of tentative early-stage planning, sensitive judgments, and data on individual employees. Likewise, in these days of tight budgets no one expects the MDBs to spend large amounts of money publishing and disseminating all the documents they write. However, the Task Force believes that major MDB operating documents should be available upon request to citizens of member countries. These documents include the following:

- ❑ Final-stage institutional planning and budget documents, so that all concerned can know the bank's future plans and the quality of argumentation buttressing them.

- ❑ Full information on future projects, so that all who will be affected will be aware of what is planned and can make additional information known to the bank. In contrast to the current situation where much information on projects being designed is confidential, the MDBs should actively seek to disseminate information on upcoming projects to encourage local input and discussion (exceptions would be proprietary information or matters concerning a member's national security). A basic project description should be available in at least one local language. This seems particularly important given that lack of accurate local information appears to have been a problem in failures of a number of past projects.

- ❑ Information on the status of ongoing projects and the results of past projects. This would include terms of reference for major contracts and curricula vitae of key contractors. If sensitive information (i.e., allegations of malfeasance against specific individuals) is contained in these documents, it could be put in a confidential addendum (i.e., not released). (The ADB currently makes available to the public all of its project completion reports and project evaluations.)

Processes. In addition to document transparency, the MDBs, as institutions supported by taxpayers in both developed and developing countries, need to conduct their business and make major decisions on their future role and policies in a way that maintains public support and trust. This means that major decisions on future institutional directions and policies should be regarded as matters of legitimate taxpayer interest and, when such interest is apparent, the MDBs should attempt to provide interested parties with clear and complete information. In cases where members of the public have both an evident interest in and professional knowledge of a major topic under discussion, it makes sense for the MDB to try to obtain and take advantage of the concerned group's information and views.

This is obviously an area in which senior MDB officials will need to exercise good judgment. The banks make thousands of operational decisions annually, and the intent of this recommendation is not to impose a burdensome requirement for public disclosure about all such decisions, most of which may be of no interest to the public. On the other hand, when significant numbers of concerned groups or individuals want information on an upcoming bank decision or policy choice, in view of the institutions' public nature and dependence on public support for cooperation in operational activities in borrowing countries and for funding in developed countries, the MDBs should not refuse to provide relevant information. Indeed, for the most important MDB policy decisions that will affect the nature and quality of future operations, the MDBs should routinely make available information on their policy proposals in advance of final decisions and, where relevant, seek the views of knowledgeable outside groups.

In view of the importance that MDB country lending strategies are assuming in the analysis of country conditions and the planning of future MDB operations, these documents should be made available to the public substantially before they are considered by the MDB's board. The Task Force shares the view put forward in the study funded by the Danish International Development Agency in 1991, but believes that the conclusions regarding public availability of country strategies should apply to all the MDBs as well as the World Bank:

> The World Bank is the multilateral agency with by far the strongest analytical capacity to prepare coherent country strategies and programmes. Still, it does not engage in public and joint programming exercises with the recipient governments. The Study Team had the opportunity to study the country strategy papers for three of the case countries, and is convinced that they could have served as an ideal foundation for policy dialogues with the governments and as an excellent reference framework for other donors operating in the country. The governments of most developing countries are now so strong that they can cope with frank, well-prepared Bank views on development constraints, etc. in their country.... The secrecy tends to confirm the image of the Bank as an omnipotent agency and reduces its capacity to learn from mistakes and from alternative perspectives.[45]

Problems posed by the "reformatting" of operational directives in the World Bank. This has become a center of controversy recently as the World Bank has sought to make clear which parts of some of its operational policies should be considered by staff to be binding "operational directives," which are the also binding "bank procedures," and which fall into the not binding category of "best practice" suggestions to staff. Because a number of these policies had been negotiated in the last few years in the World Bank's Board, with strong input from various U.S. nongovernmental groups, the fact that the Bank apparently has chosen to

---

45. Danida, Danish Ministry of Foreign Affairs, *Effectiveness of Multilateral Agencies at Country Level* (Denmark: Danida, 1991), 2.28.

determine internally which parts of these documents it would consider binding, without sending the clarified documents back to the Executive Board for approval, has aroused much concern. (In a number of cases it appears that the content of the binding portions of the "reformatted policies" is significantly weaker than the policy documents they are attempting to "clarify.") At stake also is the part of these policies that is subject to examination by the World Bank Inspection Panel, which does not have jurisdiction over failure to abide by standards that the Bank terms as merely "good practice." After several discussions, it appeared to the Task Force that this practice represents a retreat from a reasonably open and transparent discussion on these policies held several years ago to a far less transparent reformulation of these policies into binding and nonbinding parts, without either consistent outside knowledge and consultation or approval by the executive directors.

> **RECOMMENDATION 14. MDB Operations: Transparency.** The MDBs should change their policies on the public availability of documents to make many more documents public information, in many instances before final decisions on them are made, as noted previously for specific types of documents.
>
> The MDBs should acknowledge as legitimate the interest of citizens of all shareholder countries in their key decisions, seeking to keep them informed of upcoming major policy choices about which they evince interest and, where they have useful experience or information, taking their concerns into account.
>
> **BENCHMARK.** *The MDBs have changed their public information policies and practices along the above lines.*
>
> *The World Bank is consulting with concerned groups as it "reformats its operational directives," and where there are divergent views on what aspects of policy documents should be mandatory requirements, these are referred to the Executive Board.*

EVALUATING PERFORMANCE OF THE MDBs: Determining Results of Bank Projects

MDB Evaluation Systems: What Others Say

...there often is uneven recognition of the need for creditable evaluation data and analyses to respond to legitimate questions of and faced by MDB contributors. Most have to go to their elected legislatures to secure appropriations of funds for the MDBs. In the past, general statements of MDB relevance may have been sufficient. The end of the Cold War, publicized MDB failures, and budget constraints now make it tougher to secure support. The MDBs need to respond to issues concerning effectiveness.... To put it bluntly, neither the Congress nor the administration really can say with certainty that varied MDB policies and programs are succeeding or not succeeding. Similarly, neither the business community nor the academic community can readily determine the effect or effectiveness of MDB initiatives.[46]

Marshall Kaplan
The MDBs and Evaluation: A U.S. Perspective

It has been MDB policy since the mid 1970s to promote monitoring and evaluation (M&E) of project implementation…overall results of the 20 year M&E initiative have been disappointing…the history of M&E in the Bank is characterized by non-compliance.[47]

World Bank Operations Evaluation Department
June 30, 1994

That an average of over US$5 billion a year for each of the past five years can have been spent in the name of achieving development for people in poverty without a mechanism for assessing whether it does them harm or good is an indictment of the political management of, and accountability for, aid. It underlines the need for a strong new policy commitment to poverty eradication, proper objective setting and the rigorous evaluation of performance against poverty objectives.[48]

The Reality of Aid 1996: An Independent Review of International Aid

Background

In the post–Cold War world where simply funneling money into problem areas is a discredited option, it is critical that the MDBs have a credible system to evaluate the results of their expenditures and share these results with their shareholders. Because the United States must make difficult choices in a tight budget environment, it is important that the MDBs find a way to convincingly show improved results from their programs. Given the multistage U.S. decisionmaking process on MDB funding, it also is important that the information on MDB program results be available not just to a few administration officials, but broadly to Congress and interested citizen groups. In devising a process to demonstrate their results, the MDBs should bear in mind that both internal and external studies have shown a mixed track record of program success and their evaluation systems are likely to face critical scrutiny. Untransparent systems that require reader trust in many internal judgments are likely to have difficulty engendering confidence.

---

46. Marshall Kaplan, "The MDBs and Evaluation: A U.S. Perspective" (paper prepared for the CSIS Task Force on the United States and the MDBs, Washington, D.C., October 22, 1996), 2.

47. World Bank, Operations Evaluation Department, *An Overview of Monitoring and Evaluation in the World Bank* (Washington, D.C.: World Bank, June 30, 1994), cited by Jonathan Fox, "Promoting Independent Assessments of MDB Poverty Reduction Investments: Bringing Civil Society In" (paper prepared for the CSIS Task Force on the United States and the MDBs, Washington, D.C., July 12, 1996), 3.

48. Nancy Alexander, "World Bank's Loan Portfolio Management: How Reforms Can Reduce Poverty" (paper prepared for the CSIS Task Force on the United States and the MDBs, Washington, D.C., August 11, 1996), 17.

MDB evaluation systems are not designed to provide needed information to shareholders. Existing MDB evaluation systems are not designed to and do not provide shareholders with the kind of information they need to make informed judgments about the effectiveness of bank programs. Most current MDB evaluation systems are directed at providing information internally to bank officers and staff and, to some degree, to borrowing-country officials. Clearly, both of these audiences are very important, as are the objectives of internal self-criticism and learning. However, such internally focused "practitioner-directed" systems do not provide the accountability needed to demonstrate that the MDBs are using public funds effectively.

Current MDB evaluative material does not adequately inform outside observers for the following reasons:

❐ It may still largely focus on whether funds were expended or inputs procured in a timely way, rather than on whether substantive development objectives were achieved and benefits accrued to those intended. (Some banks, especially the World Bank, have moved beyond this point to have more sophisticated, results-focused systems.)

❐ Much of the results of MDB evaluations are not available to the public or are available only in highly sanitized form.

❐ Evaluation systems are so cumbersome and slow (with evaluative material becoming available years after project disbursements have ceased) that the institutions normally claim that weaknesses shown have long since been corrected. Whether or not such claims are credible, they are hard to dispute if the projects evaluated were closed years before.

❐ Results, when they are made available to the public, tend to be presented in a way that makes it difficult even for experts to make judgments. Either evaluations are presented on an extremely detailed basis (70–100 pages written on a project), where enormous amounts of time are required to assemble enough data to get a meaningful sense of an MDB's track record, or, more commonly, the only information provided to the public is some sort of compendium of evaluation results, where complex methodologies and reluctance to identify specific projects and countries make it hard for outsiders to draw meaningful conclusions.

Quality of MDB evaluation information varies. Going beyond the issue of whether the MDBs are providing enough information and the right kind of material to shareholders, it appears that the quality of the various MDBs' evaluation efforts differs markedly, as do the methodologies they use. The World Bank's Operations Evaluation Department (OED), which reports directly to the institution's Board of Directors rather than to the Bank's president or other internal officials, is noteworthy for the high analytical quality of its reports and for its willingness to make tough judgments on Bank operations. In spite of the World Bank evaluation system's internal focus, the question is often asked whether sufficient use is made by the Bank of the high-quality analysis that is generated. Several of the other MDBs' evaluation material appears extremely bland in comparison, with judgments tempered so as not to give offense, thus making it even more difficult to get information about development results.

In looking at the kind of MDB evaluation system that would meet shareholders' needs, an effort should be made to build on, and certainly safeguard, the analytical quality and independence of the World Bank OED system, while making the results more available and useful to shareholders. The analytical quality of the efforts of the other institutions should be upgraded. (The EBRD had just begun to have enough completed projects for useful evaluation results to be available.)

Change Needed

All of the MDBs need to put in place a system that provides credible information about what the results have been of the public funds they have expended. This task is not simple because it involves judgments about what could reasonably have been expected from a project and about the importance of some causal factors compared with others. Likewise, MDB evaluation reports need to strike a difficult balance between encouragement of innovation and risk taking (because development is not an exact science) and excessive tolerance for MDB inaction in the face of repeated problems leading to failed projects.

Given the existing skepticism in many quarters about the results of MDB projects, however, the difficulties in the evaluation process argue for the MDBs to devote more high-quality talent to the effort now, rather than to delay due to concerns about methodological challenges.

The MDBs' evaluation systems should produce information that is

- ☐ Comprehensive, covering the bulk of the MDB's lending program, because the objective is to assure shareholders that funds are well spent.

- ☐ Public. All regular MDB evaluation products should be available to the public, because taxpayers of either donor or borrowing countries are paying for the projects. If evaluations remain confidential, their utility as vehicles of public accountability is limited. The often-heard concern that evaluators will not be honest if evaluations are made public should be dealt with by appropriate MDB senior-management actions and incentives.

- ☐ Verifiable. Reports of results should identify specific projects so that independent observers can check whether they agree with the bank's conclusions in specific cases.

- ☐ Available on a timely basis. The MDBs ought to be able to produce at least brief reports on the results of all projects that were completed in the last 12–18 months, so that results are not outdated when received.

- ☐ Clear in its judgments, for which the evaluation system can be held accountable, on whether projects achieved objectives and were effective uses of the funds expended.

❏ Clear in its judgment of whether benefits went to the groups that were supposed to receive them.

❏ User friendly. Evaluations should use clear methodologies and present results in an easily understood way, highlighting the most important findings.

Finally, it is not credible in most cases for the MDB staff who designed and oversaw the implementation of a project to be the ones to pronounce on its success of failure. An evaluation entity that is independent of the MDB's operating staff is important to get unbiased judgments that will hold up to increased public scrutiny. Likewise, devoting some of the institution's top talent to evaluation makes sense in view of the importance of those judgments for the institution's credibility and shareholder support.

The kind of reporting that would satisfy some of the Task Force's concerns would be an annual public report on the results of all projects that had concluded disbursement in the previous year. This report would look briefly but specifically at what each project—specified by country and project title—had accomplished in comparison to its objectives and the funds spent. It would also include a summary judgment of the degree of project success, a judgment for which the MDB's evaluation system could be held accountable. Where projects had not achieved major objectives, the reasons would be noted.

Senior World Bank officials indicate that the World Bank might be prepared to produce such a report. (In the case of the World Bank, the existing "Evaluation Memoranda" prepared on all projects probably would meet this requirement if they became publicly available.) There are obviously major advantages to all the MDBs producing comparable evaluative material that would permit comparisons among institutions and help to ensure that no institution established a system designed to skew results in its favor.

Because credible information on MDB program results is so important, if some or all of the MDBs cannot develop systems meeting these criteria in one to two years, interested shareholders, if they still wished to support the MDB, should consider forming an independent MDB evaluation group, not located in any of the MDBs, that utilizes independent experts to evaluate the programs of the MDBs that have not established adequate systems of their own.

RECOMMENDATION 15. Evaluating Performance of the MDBs: Determining Results of Bank Projects. The MDBs should have evaluation systems that produce high-quality, independent judgments on whether bank programs achieved their objectives. This material should be comprehensive, verifiable, timely, reasonably user friendly, and include best judgments on whether projects achieved objectives and benefited those intended. It should be available to the public.

BENCHMARK. *Each MDB has in place a system that meets these criteria, and an examination of its products inspires confidence in the analytical quality and independent judgment of the system.*

EVALUATING PERFORMANCE OF THE MDBs: Tracking Sustainability

Background

Currently, the MDBs stop focusing on most of their projects after loan funds are disbursed (usually when the project is supposed to be fully operational). They can do this because the repayment of the loan is guaranteed by the government of the borrowing country. Exceptions are the majority of EBRD and IFC projects, which involve private borrowers without a government guarantee, and the small minority of IDB and ADB loans to private entities. In these cases, the MDB must track project progress after loan disbursement due to concern about whether the loan will be repaid.

In addition, some of the MDBs (e.g., the World Bank) study a small percentage (10–15 percent) of their loans' impact about five years after the final loan disbursement. For the vast majority of MDB projects, however, the MDBs themselves, and certainly their shareholders, have no reliable way of finding out whether MDB projects continue in operation and achieve success or failure after the MDB's resources have been disbursed

Change Needed

Because the MDBs' role is long-term development, not short-term relief, shareholders should receive information about the fate of MDB projects after external inputs cease. In addition, the predictable need to supply such information should increase both the MDBs' and borrowers' attention to the likely sustainability of project benefits as they are selecting, formulating, and implementing projects.

Although methodologically rigorous, in-depth analysis of the impact of MDB projects is desirable, such studies are very time consuming and expensive. Therefore, rather than recommend that the MDBs do a small number of intensive studies of project impact several years after external funding has ceased, the Task Force believes that the interest of MDB accountability for sustained results is better served if the MDBs report briefly every five years on the operational status and apparent outcome of a large selection of completed projects.

> **RECOMMENDATION 16. Evaluating Performance of the MDBs: Tracking Sustainability.** The MDBs should report at least every five years on the status of their projects on which disbursements ceased within the preceding five years.

> **BENCHMARK.** *The MDBs have developed a system for reporting at least every five years on the status of projects completed in the preceding five years. These reports should be country- and project-specific and describe the status of the major activities and initiatives supported by the project. Where possible, the reports should discuss the impact of the project and the groups that benefited.*

U.S. FINANCIAL SUPPORT: Approach to Determining U.S. Financial Participation

Background

The Task Force deliberately did not consider the question of U.S. financial support for the MDBs until after coming to conclusions on the role they should be playing and their performance in important areas, believing that such substantive considerations should be the determining factor in deciding upon budget allocations.

It should also be noted that reduced administration commitments for new replenishments over the last two years resulted in decreases in annual budget authority needed to fulfill them.

Change Needed

The Task Force considered three general options on U.S. financial contributions that would flow from different perceptions of the extent to which the MDBs are serving U.S. interests.

OPTION 1. No New U.S. Contributions. Due to changes in international circumstances, the MDBs either are no longer serving U.S. interests, are no longer needed, or do not need additional funds to fulfill needed functions. The United States should cease new contributions. The banks would continue to operate using reflows and income. This would affect MDB concessional windows most, because a number of MDB capital windows do not need additional funding.

Advantages.

- Would save money.

- (Advantage or disadvantage depending on perspective.) Lack of support from the United States would make the MDBs decline in relative importance over time. Donors would likely shift new resources to programs not necessarily preferred by the United States (e.g., to EU aid vehicles).

Disadvantages.

- United States would lose influence and accumulated privileges (e.g., naming the president of the World Bank and other MDB senior officials) and probably some procurement rights.

- United States would be sharply criticized and perceived by many as not fulfilling its world-leadership obligations.

- Given their large capital base, the MDBs would continue to exist as sizable international economic entities, but would have less impetus for reform and would be immune to U.S. influence.

- If loss of U.S. financial support were to lead to a sharp decline in new lending, some countries might refuse to repay old loans, which could imperil the institutions' financial solvency.

- World would lack broadly supported international entity to coordinate aid donors and to take the lead on international development issues (e.g., reconstruction of Bosnia, development in the West Bank/Gaza, global environmental concerns).

OPTION 2. United States Maintains Higher Previous Levels of Support in Real Terms. The MDBs serve the continuing U.S. foreign policy interest of channeling resources to friendly governments. They buttress and facilitate U.S. world leadership, and the United States receives substantial commercial benefits from its leading role in them. Their performance in achieving programmatic objectives is either adequate or irrelevant, especially in light of the significant U.S. leadership interests that they serve. The United States should participate financially at about currently negotiated levels, to be adjusted upward in the future as necessary to take account of inflation.

Advantages.

- Support for this option would be popular internationally. It would keep the MDBs from becoming an issue either with allies or other developing countries.

- Would maintain U.S. leadership position in the institutions, including U.S. ability to fill key slots and U.S. veto power over some IDB lending.

- U.S. companies would benefit from procurement.

Disadvantages.

- Would require budget expenditures of $1.3 billion to $1.4 billion per year.

- Unclear how it would work out in terms of leveraging significant changes in the institutions. Given complacent attitude of other shareholders and institutional inertia, achieving major reforms could be an uphill struggle. Without changes in MDBs, funds might continue to flow to countries with poor policies, thus undercutting country-policy reforms.

OPTION 3. U.S. Links Level of Support to Performance of Each MDB. The degree to which MDBs are in the U.S. interest depends heavily upon their performance in a range of areas important to the United States. Due to changes in the international political and economic arenas, the results of MDB programs assume particularly great importance. The United States should base its financial contribution on the extent of mutual agreement with other bank shareholders on objectives, and on performance in these areas, based on bank-by-bank scrutiny and on resource needs for lending programs consistent with these objectives.

Advantages.

- Could provide significant leverage for changes in MDBs.

- Implementation of this option through the ability to suspend contributions during the annual appropriations process should guard against wasteful use of resources for MDBs pursuing low-priority programs or operating ineffectively.

- Would establish for international community clear and reasonable benchmarks against which U.S. MDB contributions would be determined.

Disadvantages.

- Would require tough negotiations with other shareholders and MDB managements on a variety of difficult issues.

- Effective implementation would require continued monitoring of MDB performance and updating U.S. views on what the priorities should be.

- Could lead to increased tensions with other countries over judgments as to which reforms to undertake and whether agreed-upon reforms had been implemented.

- If MDBs perform well, significant funding could be needed for some institutions.

Approximately 13 percent of Task Force members are in favor of Option 1, 15 percent in favor of Option 2, and 72 percent in favor of Option 3.

U.S. FINANCIAL SUPPORT: Expectations on Timing of Reforms

Background

Although many Task Force members support the Recommendation 17 third option, which would base U.S. financial contributions to individual MDBs on the institution's performance in key areas, there is a difference in view about how to implement this option. The difference primarily concerns the time frame within which the implementation of new reforms would be expected to take place.

Some Task Force members believe that the United States should pay as scheduled all funds committed under MDB replenishments that have already been negotiated, provided that all provisions of those replenishment agreements are met.

Some of the reforms sought by Task Force members are mentioned in these agreements, but in many cases replenishment-agreement language is not clear or specific, and ways to check progress are not specified. The exception to this is the AfDF agreement, which is tranched to allow checking on whether promises are kept. (Appendix E shows to what degree IDA 11, the fourth ADB General Capital

Increase, and the AfDF 7 agreements contain provisions similar to Task Force recommendations.)

For reforms that might be called for but are not included in these replenishment agreements, the administration would be asked to try to negotiate provisions in new replenishments that might cover these matters. These could be operative if and when an IDA 12 agreement comes into effect (probably July 1999) and when an AfDF 8 enters into force (probably also in 1999). (It is not clear whether the ADB will ever need a new capital increase, and the EBRD has said that it would not expect to seek one.)

Other Task Force members believe that it is reasonable to make decisions on the priority of funding for various MDBs as early as the next fiscal year's budget, based on progress toward implementing reforms along the lines suggested by the Task Force. Those holding this view point out that U.S. MDB replenishment negotiating teams are only empowered to make "qualified commitments" to new replenishments. These "qualified commitments" are not legally binding until approved by congressional action.

Two Variations on How Soon to Implement Performance-Based Funding Option

> **VARIATION 1.** The United States should support MDB replenishments that have already been negotiated by the administration (IDA 11, the EBRD capital increase, the initial subscription to the Middle East Development Bank, and replenishments of the concessional windows of the African Development Bank and the Asian Development Bank) at negotiated levels so long as negotiated replenishment conditions are met. However, for new replenishments the United States should base its decisions about financial participation on progress toward internationally negotiated reforms along the lines recommended.

> **VARIATION 2.** The United States should determine its financial participation in the MDBs on the basis of progress toward the specified reforms, beginning with the next fiscal year's budget. For replenishments that have been negotiated but not yet authorized by Congress, actions of the MDBs toward implementing these reforms should be considered in deciding upon authorizations. Institutions successfully pursuing reforms along these lines should receive priority in annual budget appropriations.

Approximately 75 percent of the Task Force members support the first variation; approximately 25 percent of the Task Force members support the second variation.

In order to facilitate consideration of new replenishments, the administration should provide a statement concerning the degree to which such replenishment agreements or other initiatives include specific actions to achieve improved performance and institutional reform along the lines suggested in this report.

IMPLEMENTATION OF RECOMMENDATIONS

Throughout the Task Force's discussions, the question kept arising as to whether, given their multilateral nature, recommendations for the MDBs could ever be implemented even if the various schools of U.S. thought could reach agreement on future directions for these institutions. It is obvious that many of the recommendations made by the group are beyond the ability of MDB managements to implement on their own and will require the acquiescence, and preferably the support, of a significant number of other shareholders.

It should be noted, however, that none of the recommendations spring from a narrow U.S. national interest. They are not designed to secure advantages for U.S. individuals or firms and reflect only the most broad political motivations. The Task Force strongly believes that these recommendations are as much in the interests of citizens of the borrowing countries and taxpayers in other donor countries as they are those of the United States.

Therefore, the Task Force urges both the executive and the legislative branches of the U.S. government to talk to their counterparts in other MDB member countries about these recommendations, solicit their views (making modifications when others have better ideas), and try to move forward with others who have similar views to implement the recommendations. Not only can executive-branch officials pursue their contacts, but legislative groups also can do much to explain our concerns and the basis for our proposals to their counterparts in other legislative bodies, which in many cases are becoming both more interested in and more influential on these issues in their countries. U.S. officials dealing with the MDBs should seek to facilitate forums in which legislative-branch members can discuss these issues with foreign counterparts. Likewise, corporate and private Task Force members can assist in this effort in a less official way through private conversations and contacts.

It would certainly be useful if other MDB member countries performed additional research or developed their own proposals to address the concerns raised by this group. This would serve to enrich and expand the dialogue, and probably to foster better solutions.

After the issues have been debated and enough time has elapsed to allow changes to be made, however, the United States will have to decide whether the collective efforts in each MDB have resulted in a product that is a priority for the expenditure of U.S. resources.

U.S. Funding of the MDBs[49]

The World Bank Group

International Bank for Reconstruction and Development (IBRD)

The total amount of paid-in capital that was owed by the United States for the 1988 General Capital Increase (GCI) was $421 million; of this, the final amount was appropriated in FY 1996.

International Development Association (IDA)

IDA funding is structured in three-year replenishment cycles, and IDA X was concluded on June 30, 1996. The total U.S. pledge for IDA X was $3.750 billion. The United States still owes $234.5 million toward IDA X.

A new IDA replenishment was negotiated in spring 1996, which includes a two-year commitment for the United States of $800 million annually beginning in FY 1998. The administration's FY 1998 budget request includes both this payment to IDA XI plus the $234.5 million owed to IDA X.

International Finance Corporation (IFC)

IFC received a GCI in 1991. The total pledged U.S. contribution was $247.5 million, and the final U.S. payment was appropriated in FY 1997.

Multilateral Investment Guarantee Agency (MIGA)

MIGA is continuing to use capital subscribed in its initial capitalization negotiated in 1988 and for which the U.S. payment was appropriated in 1988.

MIGA now is exploring prospects for an increase in its capitalization, both paid-in and callable, but discussions are not yet concluded.

Global Environment Facility (GEF)

GEF is currently in the third year of a four-year replenishment cycle. The total U.S. pledge was $430 million; through FY 1997 a total of $190 million (or 44 percent) has been appropriated. The FY 1998 budget requests $100 million for GEF.

Discussions have begun on a new replenishment, and the World Bank hopes agreement will be reached by the end of 1997.

---

49. As of September 1997 when conclusions of the Task Force were announced.

Inter-American Development Bank (IDB)

Hard Window (Ordinary and Inter-Regional Capital): In 1994, member countries agreed on an eighth replenishment, after which the institution may not need further capital increases. The United States agreed to provide $153 million in paid-in capital over six years. Of this amount, $76.8 million (or 50 percent) has been appropriated. An additional $25.6 million is being requested in FY 1998.

For the same replenishment, the United States agreed to pay $82.3 million over four years to the IDB's soft window, the Fund for Special Operations (FSO). Of this, $40.9 million (or 49.7 percent) has been appropriated. $20.6 million is being requested in FY 1998.

The United States pledged $51 million to the Inter-American Investment Corporation's initial capitalization. This obligation was settled in FY 1995, and no further funding increases have been negotiated.

The United States agreed to pay $500 million to the Multilateral Investment Fund (MIF) over five years beginning in FY 1991. With the FY 1997 appropriation of $27.5 million, a total of $321.2 million (or about 64 percent) has been paid. For FY 1998 an additional $30 million has been requested.

Asian Development Bank (ADB)

The ADB is in its fourth year of a capital replenishment that doubled its capital base and is expected to fund lending for five years.

The United States has agreed to pay the bank $66.6 million in paid-in capital over six years beginning in FY 1996; of this, it has paid $26.4 million (or 40 percent). An additional $13.2 million is requested in the FY 1998 budget.

The United States pledged $680 million to the fifth Asian Development Fund (ADF) replenishment, which covered lending through 1996. The United States has paid $443 million (or about 65 percent).

The administration just agreed to contribute $400 million to a sixth ADF replenishment to cover lending in 1997–2000.

The administration is requesting $150 million in ADF funding in the FY 1998 budget—$50 million to pay toward U.S. arrears from the fifth replenishment and $100 million for the first U.S. payment to the sixth replenishment.

African Development Bank (AfDB)

The fifth AfDB GCI is currently under negotiation. No funding is requested in the FY 1998 budget.

Donor support for the African Development Fund (AfDF) has been provided in three-year replenishment cycles. A seventh AfDF replenishment was agreed upon in 1996. The United States pledged $200 million over three years. The FY 1998 budget request contains $50 million for the initial installment.

European Bank for Reconstruction and Development (EBRD)

Negotiations were completed in 1996 for what is expected to be the first and final capital increase for the EBRD. The FY 1998 budget request contains $35.8 million for the first of eight payments for the U.S. share of the increase.

Existing MDB Programs in Support of Private Projects[50]

The oldest and largest of these programs, managed by the International Finance Corporation (IFC), a World Bank affiliate, provided $2.5 billion in loans and $618.8 million in equity and quasi-equity investments in FY 1996 (compared with $21.5 billion in commitments from the IBRD/IDA, virtually all of which went to public-sector borrowers). IFC typically limits its financing to 25 percent of the total project cost (debt and equity), usually $5 to $125 million per project, for an average of $60 million. IFC's need for project and country diversification precludes providing much more financing for a single project. The other World Bank private-sector affiliate, the Multilateral Investment Guarantee Agency (MIGA), provides political-risk insurance against narrowly defined risks. MIGA is even more circumscribed (project limits of $50 million; country limits at $225 million) and currently has almost exhausted its unused guarantee authority.

The World Bank itself can only provide loans or loan guarantees that receive a borrowing-government guarantee, which significantly limits their utility in private transactions. In spite of repeated rhetoric and efforts to make the World Bank private-sector guarantee program more useful and user friendly for private projects, only nine loan guarantees have been provided since the inception of the program in 1994 (three of them in FY 1996, and one thus far in FY 1997).

The IDB, the ADB, and the AfDB all have quite small and limited programs to provide loans or equity to private projects without a government guarantee or to make guarantees for funding for private-sector projects.

The IDB, in its private-sector operations, including the guarantee program, has two limitations: (1) no more than 5 percent of the IDB's estimated annual lending program may be allocated to finance projects in the private sector without government guarantees, and (2) the IDB's share of any individual project may not exceed 25 percent of total cost or the equivalent of $75 million, whichever is less. In FY 1995, the IDB provided $145 million in loans without a government guarantee, but made no loan guarantees.

Instead of setting a percentage limit on private-sector operations, the ADB has been allocating specific amounts of resources for such operations. During the four-year period from 1992 to 1995, the ADB approved a total of $19.6 billion for loan and equity investments, of which $513.5 million (or 2.6 percent) was used for private-sector operations. In FY 1995, the ADB provided $86.5 million in loans

---

50. Status report as of December 1996.

and $110.4 million in equity without a government guarantee, and $142 million in guarantees.

In FY 1996, the AfDB provided $23 million in loans without a government guarantee, but made no loan guarantees.

APPENDIX C

Partnerships to Expand MDB Capacity

Even if the MDBs substantially strengthen their capacity to know what is going on in borrowing countries, they are not likely ever to have the direct capacity to carry out or even oversee on a detailed basis the "retail work of development." In many cases, borrowing governments do this—checking, for example, to see that local health posts are operating, drugs are on the shelves, staff is on site, and needy people are receiving services. In other cases, however, the borrowing government cannot or will not adequately play this role. In these cases, the MDBs can try to fill the gap by finding an appropriate partner to take charge of detailed local work and oversight.

In "Wholesalers Who Need Retail Outlets," his contribution to the Mott Foundation's 1996 book on *What's Ahead for the World Bank*, World Bank official Ian Johnson (assistant CEO of the Global Environment Facility) discussed this issue:

> The Bank can't set out the rhetoric of the new agenda and be as centralized as it is. If the corporate decision of the Bank is that it's not going to decentralize, it has to be creative at finding intermediaries to do its work. That's going to be a big challenge.
>
> I don't mean handing more money to NGOs. Finding real intermediaries that are closer to the ground is going to be a really important part of the new agenda. The GEF and the Bank are wholesalers and they need to find retail outlets.... We've got to find somebody who can carry the ball....[51]

In addition to helping design and implement projects, in some circumstances local partners can help MDBs monitor project progress by providing an independent voice about how projects are going. Professor Jonathan Fox noted in his paper for the Task Force:

> One of the main advantages of independent M&E units [local groups monitoring MDB projects] is their capacity to cross-check official data with field evidence and by speaking directly to ostensible beneficiaries. This is crucial for assessing the difference between services delivered on paper and in practice. For example, water pipes may have been installed, but that does not mean that water is flowing in them. Schools may be built, but lack teachers or books. Clinics may be open, but staff may be abusive or absent. This process involves

---

51. Ian Johnson, "Wholesalers Who Need Retail Outlets," *What's Ahead for the World Bank* (Flint, Mich.: Charles Stewart Mott Foundation, 1996), 29.

surveying nonbeneficiaries as well, to find out who may have been excluded and why. Compared with other kinds of MDB-funded projects, such as larger infrastructure investments, antipoverty projects are especially difficult to assess because of their highly disaggregated and decentralized nature.[52]

Variety of Potential Partners

There are a number of possible entities that could serve as partners for the MDBs in field-level work:

❏ Private nonprofit organizations (NGOs). These groups now provide 14 percent of all development assistance and their ranks are growing rapidly. It is estimated that there are 18,000 registered nongovernmental organizations (NGOs) in the Philippines and 3,000 in Brazil; in India registered NGOs handle $520 million a year, or 25 percent of all external aid.[53]

❏ Local or international foundations.

❏ Local universities or research institutes, possibly working in partnership with similar organizations from developed countries.

❏ For-profit entities. As an example, the retail work of providing family-planning services has long been backstopped for some donors by especially created for-profit firms under long-term contracts. These firms bear the brunt of the supervisory responsibility for on-the-ground services.

❏ Other public institutions (such as UNICEF or IFAD) with an appropriate specialized focus.

Impact Dependent on Partners Chosen and Quality of Interaction

However useful in theory MDB partnerships with groups with strong local networks might be, in practice whether partnerships help a bank to achieve objectives depends upon the partners selected and upon the bank's relationship to the partners.

First, the partner must have the capacity to play its role. More difficult to ascertain, the partner must fully support the objectives of the project. Especially in poverty-reduction projects, the partner needs to represent the interests of planned beneficiaries, not those of other local groups. Discerning the interests represented by various local groups is often not easy. Sometimes elites control groups pretending to represent the disadvantaged, and some supposedly nongovernmental groups

---

52. Jonathan Fox, "Promoting Independent Assessments of MDB Poverty Reduction Investments: Bringing Civil Society In" (paper prepared for the CSIS Task Force on the United States and the MDBs, Washington, D.C., July 1996), 4.

53. *NGOs and the [World] Bank: Incorporating FY 95 Progress Report on Cooperation Between the World Bank and NGOs* (Washington, D.C.: World Bank, 1996), 1.

can be alter egos of the government. David Hunter of the Center for International Environmental Law (CIEL) discusses the difficulty in sorting out local allegiances in a 1996 article:

> For example, the Pehuen Foundation established as part of the IFC-financed Pangue Dam on the BioBio River in Chile, was one of the first such projects in Latin America and has recently been cited as a model by the Bank staff. Yet, outside critics argue that the foundation's structure is not independent, that it is being used to promote the agenda of Chile's major electrical utility, and that it is not responsive to community needs.[54]

The ability of a partner to help an MDB achieve its objectives also depends upon whether the relationship between the bank and the partner is appropriate to achieving the desired results. For example, if a local partner's role is to be sure a project is suitable to local conditions, it can only do this if it has an early and significant role in selecting and designing the project. Likewise, a local partner that is supposed to assure effective implementation of a project would need broad authority and firm support from the MDB to make midcourse corrections and take a tough stand when problems threaten project success.

Are Current MDB Structures Suited to Productive Partnerships?

Some Task Force members knowledgeable in this area contended that current MDB structures are not well suited to partnerships. Kevin Quigley, formerly with the Pew Foundation and the author of a book on the role of local foundations in eastern Europe, in a paper for the World Bank, wrote

> At the moment the [World] Bank is not well-structured to take advantage of the strengths that the NGO sector would bring to an enlarged partnership.... Even if the Bank staff are informed and committed to expanded NGO participation in Bank activities, this is often difficult to accomplish given the general lack of incentives.[55]

In a 1995 book, the University of Maryland's Paul Nelson was even more pessimistic about the expansion of meaningful partnerships between the World Bank and NGOs in the absence of major changes in Bank operations:

> While some staff members consider the Bank's "NGO Work" a passing fad, there is no doubt that the number of NGO projects has grown substantially. But as to the nature of the interaction—the terms of engagement—the record is not as favorable. For most projects NGO influence is limited to implementing a

---

54. David Hunter, *The Role of the World Bank in Strengthening Governance, Civil Society, and Human Rights* (Washington, D.C.: Center for International Environmental Law, January 1996), 13.

55. David P. Daniel, Krzyszof J. Nevs, and Kevin F. F. Quigley, "Toward Broader and More Effective NGO Participation in World Bank Activities in Eastern Europe: Two Case Studies—Poland and Slovakia" (draft paper prepared for the World Bank, Washington, D.C., 1996), 28.

component of a project designed and negotiated by World Bank staff and government officials....

The World Bank's organizational culture is hierarchical and assigns great value to specialization, technical expertise, and control of the Bank supported operations. This culture I argue is incompatible with the participatory, flexible operation that many NGOs require....

The pressure of time and money is the most discussed theme in my interviews with World Bank staff. Many cite what a senior Asia economist called "the disbursement imperative" as a key limit on innovative lending. "There is no incentive to innovate," argues one staffer, when one rises by moving money quickly.... Limited staff time per project surfaces even more often than the disbursement imperative. Working with NGOs takes time, and senior project staff from Latin America and EMENA stressed that they lack the staff to canvass and build relations with NGOs. Two Operational staff stressed the need to hold down one's "coefficients," the work-weeks per project figures reported in Project Completion Reports.[56]

Slightly different concerns led former Save the Children Federation Vice President Jim Kunder to conclude that disparities in size, expertise, and resources would limit the impact of MDB/NGO collaboration on a project-by-project basis. Therefore, he suggested in a paper prepared for the Task Force that the MDBs expand partnerships with private nonprofit donors on a priority-sector basis, structured along the lines of the Consultative Group to Assist the Poorest (CGAP) in the microenterprise area.[57] Under this model, the MDBs and private entities active in a priority sector would come together in a structured setting to learn from each other's experiences and develop means to work more closely together.

Other Task Force members believed that it would be useful for potential MDB partners to be selected on a competitive basis according to efficiency and cost-effectiveness in achieving program objectives in a particular case. In these circumstances, it would be useful to consider the merits of a wide range of groups that might have different advantages and disadvantages.

In many cases, partnerships can expand the capacity of the MDBs to achieve success in difficult and complex areas. However, the test of any partnership the MDBs choose to establish or of their decision to work alone without external partners must be project effectiveness and sustainability.

---

56. Paul Nelson, *The World Bank and Non-Governmental Organizations: The Limits of Apolitical Development* (New York: St. Martin's Press, 1995), 103–104, 176–177, 179.

57. James Kunder, "A Strategic Priority for the MDBs: Full Partnership with the Private Non-Profits" (paper prepared for the CSIS Task Force on the United States and the MDBs, Washington, D.C., 1996).

Examples of Discrepancies between MDB Policies and Performance

The following examples were provided to the Task Force by Task Force members or authors of commissioned papers or they emerged in the course of research for other recommendations.

1. Several successive internal reviews of World Bank resettlement activities have found major discrepancies from Bank policy.[58]

2. The 1992 World Bank Portfolio Management Task Force Report (the Wapenhans Report) included this information:

    > Borrowers' compliance with legal covenants is another major problem. Although only partial data are available, the evidence of gross non-compliance is overwhelming. A recent COD study showed that only 22 percent of the financial covenants in loan/credit agreements were in compliance. A recent OED study of water supply projects financed by the Bank in 1967–89 showed similar results: only 25 percent of financial covenants were in compliance. The preliminary findings of a review of compliance with financial covenants for revenue earning entities in one region shows only 15 percent of projects in full compliance.[59]

    Whether any more recent analysis has been done of compliance with World Bank project legal conditions and covenants is not known.

3. An October 1993 World Bank Task Force on Financial Reporting and Auditing found that "Compliance with audit covenants has been very mixed with weak compliance compounded by a lack of sufficient interest and understanding by Bank staff…. While over 90 percent of audited financial information is received within two years of being due, less than 40 percent is received by its due dates, making it inconsequential for project management purposes."[60]

---

58. World Bank, Environment Department, *Resettlement and Development: The Bankwide Review of Projects Involving Involuntary Resettlement 1986–1993* (Washington, D.C.: World Bank, April 8, 1994).

59. World Bank Portfolio Management Task Force, *Effective Implementation: Key to Development Impact* (Washington, D.C.: World Bank, September 22, 1992), 9.

60. World Bank, Central and Auditing Accounting Division, *Financial Reporting and Auditing Task Force Report* (Washington, D.C.: World Bank, October 8, 1993), 1.

4. In 1994, the Environmental Defense Fund and the Natural Resources Defense Council reviewed all World Bank projects in the upcoming project pipeline covered by the Bank's energy policy, which had been approved in 1992. Out of 46 power sector loans, they found that only 2 were in compliance with all aspects of the new policy.[61]

   A follow-on study (by World Wildlife Fund–Sweden) in February 1996 found that of 56 World Bank projects (both ongoing and upcoming) studied, 3 appeared to comply fully with the Bank's energy policy, 17 were judged to comply partially, and 36 were found not to comply with the policy.[62]

5. A 1994 World Bank Operations Evaluation Department review of the World Bank's experience with conditional lending in the forestry sector found a significant degree of partial compliance or noncompliance with loan covenants.[63]

6. University of Maryland research scholar Paul Nelson, who has studied the World Bank for a number of years, discusses in a 1995 book the elements of the World Bank's organizational culture and incentives that produce the gap between rhetoric/policy and practice:

   > The extreme difficulty the World Bank has in withholding loans for even the most problematic projects illustrates the strength of the mandate [to make sizable loans]. Strict procedural standards for financial and economic return of investments, as well as environmental and social measures are "finessed" when political and internal pressures require that a loan be made....
   >
   > But the most frequent response to the time/money crunch [too little time and funding for project preparation compared with excessive amounts to lend] was described by a senior Asia economist as finessing it. "Finessing it" occurs when too much is required to be done in too little time while preparing a project. One says the right things, proposes (for example) organizing the requisite number of irrigation groups, and does one's best, knowing that the work described would require much more than the time allotted....
   >
   > A second danger lies in the gap between rhetoric and performance. Theory, policy and intellectual work on "progressive themes"—women, environment, poverty, impact of adjustment on the poor, involuntary resettlement—are often substituted by World Bank representatives for changes in actual performance....
   >
   > But Bank policy with respect to project-related forced resettlement is an example of a regularly observed pattern in social and environmental fields: policy is carefully crafted but not enforced. When governments balk at

---

61. Frances Seymour, *The World Bank and Environmental Sustainability* (Washington, D.C.: World Wildlife Fund, January 1996), iv.

62. World Wildlife Fund–Sweden, *A Megawatt Saved: Implementation of the World Bank's Energy Policy* (Sweden: World Wildlife Fund, February 1996), 10.

63. Frances Seymour, *The World Bank and Environmental Sustainability* (Washington, D.C.: World Wildlife Fund, January 1996), 5.

meeting resettlement standards in full, the Bank has been extremely reluctant or unable to win compliance. Driven by a need to move money and faced with declining influence with some major borrowers, the Bank invokes borrower sovereignty and stops short of using its leverage to protect those ousted by the project.[64]

7. A January 1996 World Bank *OED Précis* summarizing a review of 41 projects in the electric power sector in Africa notes

    Often the Bank avoided penalizing borrowers that repeatedly breached lending covenants. The large loans that it approved failed to elicit even modest policy adjustments.... Borrowers' compliance with covenants was negligible in more than 60 percent of cases.[65]

8. The World Bank's Congo River Basin strategy and its Cameroon Transport Sector Loan, considered in 1996, appeared to contravene its Forest Policy. The loan was withdrawn from Executive Board consideration after it provoked major protests.

9. An internal World Bank Africa Region Task Force report, dated May 1, 1996, discusses the gap between the Bank's poverty reduction rhetoric and its practice in sub-Saharan Africa:

    For most countries, however, poverty is not adequately addressed in Country Assistance Strategies. Even for those countries where the Bank had completed a PA [Poverty Assessment], the results are not typically reflected in the strategy. Whereas the typical PA outlines the need for increased social services and income-generating activities, often emphasizing the rural areas, the typical CAS [Country Assistance Strategy] emphasizes the importance of macroeconomic stability and factors contributing to long-term growth without any explicit assessment of the effect on reducing poverty. Notably, the CASs do not exclude consideration of social services in general but do tend to minimize this consideration of the impact of these services on the poor. This tendency is, for example, reflected in the number of urban programs that the Bank is or will be supporting. In the case of Sierra Leone, plans for an urban works program include water supply and sanitation for Freetown but no plans for a rural water supply/sanitation project nor for other rural social services projects identified as important in the CAS. Consequently, although this report concludes that the PAs have done a reasonably good job of identifying the policy and strategy options that will assist the poor to become more active participants in the growth process, these options typically are not being reflected in the Bank's assistance strategies or operations....

---

64. Paul Nelson, *The World Bank and Non-Governmental Organizations: The Limits of Apolitical Development* (New York: St. Martin's Press, 1995), 90, 104, 173, 180.

65. World Bank, OED, "Bank Lending for Electric Power in Africa: Time for a Reappraisal," *OED Précis* (Washington, D.C.: World Bank, January 1996), 1, 3.

It is important to note that few projects provide for monitoring or evaluating their effects on the poor. The projects will be supervised, but many of them do not have indicators developed to evaluate whether they are helping or reaching the poor....

In those cases where the CAS has a clear strategic vision on how to achieve poverty reduction, this vision is not effectively translated into a lending program that substantially reduces poverty. The actual work program is often driven more by the Bank's structure and staffing (the skills mix) than by the priority of poverty reduction. Specifically, the lending program often drives the country business plan and the country assistance strategy, when it should be the other way around.[66]

10. A June 1996 World Bank OED study of the effectiveness of environmental assessments found that a key element in environmental assessment, prior analysis of alternative interventions, was performed in less than half of the projects studied.

11. In spite of much World Bank rhetoric about developing projects with local participation, an internal Bank report to President Wolfensohn on the status of the 20 projects singled out to be "participation flagship projects" asks whether the Bank has the "flexibility to sustain a participatory approach" and notes that "there is a lack of funding to support participatory activities...currently sufficient financing from (externally funded) trust funds has been secured, but the process has been 'time-consuming and untidy.' In general Task Managers commented that there are often difficulties in obtaining small funds for piloting participatory initiatives."[67]

12. A World Bank audit in August 1996 found that both the World Bank and the IDB probably violated their own policies as they provided over $1.6 billion to construct the troubled Yacyreta Dam on the border between Argentina and Paraguay. The power plant is scheduled for completion in 1998, with a nine-year delay at an estimated cost of $8.2 billion (59 percent cost overrun). According to this report, the World Bank was aware in the early 1980s, before construction began, of "changing economic (slower demand growth) and technological conditions making loan cancellation and a gas-based alternative more attractive." Yet "the Bank did not act decisively when confronted with the facts. Opportunities to reassess the project were wasted in spite of the recommendations made by a good quality and timely Public Investment Review in 1985." Rather, "the Bank accepted repeated violations of major covenants and continued to associate with totally unsatisfactory sector financial and operating performance."

13. The Lawyers Committee for Human Rights provided documentation in September 1996 on its efforts (unsuccessful so far in spite of extensive World Bank

---

66. World Bank, Human Resources and Poverty Division, Technical Department, Africa Region, *Taking Action for Poverty Reduction in Sub-Saharan Africa: Report of an Africa Region Task Force* (Washington, D.C.: World Bank, May 1, 1996), 101–103, 110.

67. World Bank Office Memorandum, *Second Quarterly Report on Participation Flagships* (Washington, D.C.: World Bank, June 12, 1996), 2.

proclamations about the value of local participation) to get either the Russian implementing agency or the World Bank project staff to support consultation with local civil-society groups in a key component of the Russian Legal Reform program.

14. The book *Masters of Illusion: The World Bank and the Poverty of Nations*, published in late 1996 by a reporter for environmental and scientific publications, discusses the discrepancies between World Bank policy and practice:

> It's not clear what, if any, impact the Bank's growing list of concerns and goals has had on its lending practices. Its increasing dedication to public participation, for example, is rendered nearly meaningless by its all encompassing notion of participation. The Bank does not, for example, distinguish between information sharing, social surveys, or workshops with NGOs, and what most people would regard as true "stakeholder participation" that is, joint decision making or collaborative project preparation with those directly affected by Bank projects....
>
> In 1994, the Bank's longtime treasurer, Eugene Rotberg, said, "I am not one of those who believe that the World Bank has changed over the last twenty years. I think the rhetoric has changed, the talk has changed, and maybe, at the margin, the lending has changed. However, most of the staff are not doing things differently than they did twenty or thirty years ago."
>
> [Referring to developments since 1995, a World Bank staffer is quoted]: "The cognitive dissonance between high-level pronouncements and daily practice is at an all-time high."[68]

15. In December 1996, Mexican and international NGOs protested the lack of local civil-society consultation on the new and supposedly more participatory World Bank Country Assistance Strategy for Mexico.

---

68. Catherine Caufield, *Masters of Illusion: The World Bank and the Poverty of Nations* (New York: Henry Holt and Company, 1996), 310, 328.

Examination of New MDB Replenishment Agreements

IDA 11

The International Development Association Deputies Agreement specifies the following on matters that were the subject of task force recommendations.[69]

Funding Allocations Related to Performance Including Good Governance:

Deputies emphasized that the allocation of IDA resources should be consistent with IDA's overarching goals of poverty reduction, economic growth and environmental sustainability. Allocations, therefore, should continue to be influenced primarily by each borrower's performance in respect of these goals and in project implementation. The growing scarcity of donor resources underlines the importance of lending linked to performance. The most important determinant of good performance is whether the borrower's macroeconomic and structural policies significantly contribute to the central objective of reducing poverty within a framework of good governance. Deputies asked IDA management to ensure that the method for evaluating performance adequately emphasizes these considerations. (p. 12)

Direct Bank Support for Private-Sector Projects to Be Determined in the Context of Country Lending Strategies:

Deputies encouraged IDA management to strengthen its efforts to ensure that...the Country Assistance Strategy encompasses all the Bank Group's planned activities, including those of IFC and MIGA, demonstrating how they address the country's priority development issues. (p. 4)

Measures to Assure That the Poor Benefit from Growth:

To contribute significantly to poverty reduction, macroeconomic stabilization and adjustment policies have to be complemented by structural measures to increase poor people's economic opportunities and enhance their productivity.

---

69. This replenishment agreement was concluded in April 1996. All excerpts taken from IDA Deputies' report, April 17, 1996.

Such measures include: providing further support to the agriculture and informal sectors, which are the principal sources of income for the poor; expanding poor people's—and especially poor women's—access to land, credit and information; establishing basic labor standards and working conditions; and reforming legislation and policies that disadvantage the poor. Deputies recommend that IDA's analytical work and dialogue with borrowers assess more systematically how these qualitative and structural aspects of economic growth can contribute to poverty reduction. (p. 6)

The Bank's Role in Establishing the Preconditions for Successful Microenterprise Programs:

Deputies stressed the importance of small and microenterprises and the informal sector in job creation and income generation, especially for poor women. IDA finances projects to support small enterprises in a number of countries each year. Deputies asked that IDA assess the impact of these ongoing efforts and identify opportunities for further effective action. In particular, they stated that the Country Assistance Strategy and IDA's policy dialogue should address the economic, financial, structural, legal and regulatory issues affecting small and microenterprises, in countries where this is an important development issue. (pp. 8–9)

Need to Examine How Borrowers Use Their Own Resources:

The Deputies welcomed the agreement between the World Bank and IMF to work closely with member governments to help them improve their public finances, especially by increasing attention to funding social and economic development programs and reducing non-productive spending (including excessive military expenditures) within a framework of sustainable economic growth…. The Country Assistance Strategy should indicate how IDA intends to assist the borrower to implement changes in the size and pattern of development expenditures aimed at improving poor people's access to basic services. (pp. 6–7)

Sustainable Use of Resources:

The objectives and design of IDA-financed agriculture, transport, energy, infrastructure and water supply projects should increasingly seek to ensure that resource use is ecologically and socially sustainable, as well as economically efficient, and that local people have more control over and interest in natural resources. (pp. 7–8)

Bank Programs Should Be Developed and Implemented with Local Input and Participation:

Deputies stressed that economic development and reform programs must—if they are to be legitimate and sustainable—be understood by, and broadly reflect the views of, people in the borrowing country. They noted and endorsed IDA's intensified efforts to ensure that governments seek broad participation in the design and implementation of its programs and projects…. Deputies observed that an increasing proportion of new projects incorporate participation by stakeholders and beneficiaries. Recognizing that participation enhances the quality and sustainability of development operations, they stressed that the scope and quality of participation must continue to improve and that strengthened efforts should be made to promote the participation of women. Participation, they said, should become an integral part of IDA's operations. Continued efforts to enhance the capabilities of IDA's staff in this area would help to achieve this integration. (p. 4)

Local Citizens Should Be Involved in Developing Bank Country Assistance Strategies and Related Documents:

Deputies felt that more effort is needed to increase participation in the development of country strategies and related work. They asked that in the process of preparing the Country Assistance Strategy (CAS), IDA make greater efforts to involve borrowers' governments, affected people and organizations and other donors in discussions of the issues and priorities determining the strategy…. They also recommend that IDA, particularly through its Resident Missions, encourage and assist governments to make readily available the analysis of issues and priorities in the CAS to interested groups in the country. (pp. 4–5)

The Need to Monitor the Impact of Programs on the Poor:

They (deputies) therefore noted the importance of effective monitoring of the impact of IDA's entire portfolio on the incomes and living conditions of the poor. (p. 6)

Need to Revise Internal Incentives:

Deputies reaffirmed that IDA's impact on poverty can be judged only by the results its operations achieve in the field. They stressed that high priority must continue to be given to project performance and portfolio implementation, and that IDA's internal culture and rewards should reflect this emphasis on results. (p. 10)

Need to Evaluate Results:

The Deputies noted with satisfaction that IDA has taken significant steps to better define how its projects will contribute to poverty reduction, and to monitor their results. For each new project, monitorable indicators related to its objectives are defined and recorded at the design stage. The implementation progress and final results of the project are judged against these same indicators. The new system is now being introduced and a preliminary synthesis of initial results will be included in the Annual Report on Portfolio Performance for FY

1996, to be reviewed by IDA's Executive Directors in late 1996. It is expected that by the time of the Annual Report on Portfolio Performance for FY 1997, which Executive Directors will review in late 1997, reporting on project implementation will be fully consistent with this new approach. Deputies expect that this framework will make it easier to systematically assess the achievements of IDA operations. (pp. 10–11)

Asian Development Bank General Capital Increase

Commitments that are included in capital increase documentation that relate to Task Force recommendations are the following:[70]

Selectivity in Lending to Countries Pursuing Good Policies:

Country performance evaluation, including assessment of programs on poverty reduction, is now an integral part of the Bank's planning process. The evaluation is expected to help the Bank...to ensure that the Bank's resources are provided primarily to DMCs [Developing Member Countries] that are committed to mobilizing their own resources and using them effectively for development. (p. 4)

The ongoing review has identified some common sector level issues that must be addressed to ensure project success: (I) a Developing Member Country must have a conducive policy environment that includes the interaction of economy-wide and sector policies. (p. 7)

Agreement Not to Duplicate Private Sources of Finance:

Funding for the energy sector will be provided only to projects which cannot be funded by the private sector. (p. 8)

Project Sustainability:

[Concerning physical infrastructure] The Bank's main objectives will be...(v) ensure the sustainability of facilities and services through adequate cost recovery, tariff, and financial policies; (vi) undertake sector development in an environmentally sound manner. (p. 8)

---

70. This ADB capital increase was approved by the Bank in April 1994, and U.S. participation has been authorized by Congress. All excerpts taken from the Asian Development Bank's *Report of the Board of Directors on the Increase in Authorized Capital Stock and Subscriptions Thereto*, March 1994.

Shift Away from "Moving Money," More Focus on Building Institutional Capacity, Strengthening Project Implementation, Decentralizing Operations, and the Participation of Local People:

The report of the Task Force has been circulated to the Board. Three major themes underlie the findings and recommendations of the Task Force. First the Bank has to place greater emphasis on responding to the needs of clients (i.e. DMCs). This implies a shift away from an "approval culture," in which adequate project design and attention to local needs, demands and absorptive capacity are sacrificed to achieve annual lending targets. It also means strengthening of the country focus of Bank operations, including the links among economic and sector work, programming and project design. Second, the Bank needs to pay greater attention to building institutional capacity in DMCs and fostering their commitment to Bank-assisted projects. This calls for capacity building initiatives by the Bank, as well as the involvement of DMC officials and project beneficiaries at all stages of the project cycle. Third, there needs to be more accountability within the Bank for ensuring project quality. The implications are that project implementation must be given the same priority as project processing; that Bank systems and procedures should be decentralized to permit greater flexibility and initiative; and that feedback on lessons from experience should be utilized better in programming and project design, and in implementation activities. (p. 13)

Seventh Replenishment of the African Development Fund

Agreements that are contained in the final report that relate to task force recommendations are the following:[71]

Funding Allocations Related to Performance:

The indicative lending programs, as calculated according to paragraph 16, shall not be regarded as entitlements since access to Fund resources will depend on each country's performance assessed on an annual basis by Fund management. In this context, performance shall be based on objective and transparent analysis, in particular those of competent international organizations such as the IMF and the World Bank and defined broadly as

(i)   sound economic management;

(ii)   growth with equity and poverty reduction;

(iii)   development sustainability;

(iv)   sound ADB Group country portfolio performance, and

---

71. This replenishment was authorized by Congress in 1996. All excerpts taken from the "Draft Report on the Consultative Meetings on the Seventh General Replenishment of the Resources of the African Development Fund," May 1996.

(v)   The Fund evaluates good governance based on respect for human and political rights, rule of law, freedom of information and association and participation in government, as part of the matrix on country performance.

These five indicators involve the following specific elements:

(i)   Sound Economic Management

Effective macroeconomic management, giving due consideration to sound demand management, resource mobilization, and non-inflationary growth; an enabling price and incentive framework, including trade and exchange rate policies and the environment for private investment; the quality of public expenditure programmes, including allocations for priority recurrent spending; the extent to which adequate levels of development expenditure are occurring without being crowded out by large or rising non-developmental expenditures, including military expenditures; the progress, quality and credibility of adjustment programmes (if required), including their adherence to conditions agreed with the Fund and collaborating multilateral finance agencies; and good fiscal and financial management.

(ii)   Growth with Equity and Poverty Reduction

The quality and sustainability of government policies and programmes in the basic human resources sectors of education (especially primary and informal), health (especially primary health care and nutrition), population (including family planning and child survival) and the attention given to raising the position of women and their access both to assets and to education; the development and tracking of appropriate social indicators (e.g., life expectancy, literacy, population growth and income distribution), the quality of macro-economic and sectoral policies and other programmes designed to take account of the problems of the poor (for instance, basic water supply and sanitation), and to improve their incentives and opportunities for income-generating and employment activities; government readiness to safeguard and reshape critical poverty-related spending when undergoing major stabilization or adjustment, or to target subsidies or other specific remedial programmes upon the poorest in society.

(iii)   Development Sustainability

Management of natural resources and assessment of the environmental aspects of sectoral and project activities; demonstrated commitment to pursue environmental issues, including those with longer term implications; appropriate environmental regulations and legislation; efforts for sustained improvement of the human resource base and to pursue institutional improvement and development over the longer term; and the allocation of recurrent resources, including staff, to safeguard the maintenance and efficiency of past or newly completed investments.

(iv)   Sound ADB Group Country Portfolio Performance

The attainment of project and programme objectives depends importantly on the effectiveness with which countries manage these investments. Hence, the need for a regular review of each country's portfolio in assessing the overall performance of the countries. This exercise will be based on a regular review of each country portfolio to be done in consultation with the country. It will measure each loan against progress benchmarks established in the loan document and assign a rating for each loan. A composite rating will then be assigned to each country portfolio. In this regard, special attention shall be given to the use of objective criteria by which the success of projects and programmes will be judged. The Fund will be able to cancel nonperforming loans for redeployment; priority would be given to increase allocations to strongly performing countries.

(v)   Commitment to Good Governance

Issues such as democratization, pluralism, respect for human rights and freedom of association play an important role in determining the conditions for balanced and sustainable development.

The Fund evaluates good governance based on respect for human and political rights, rule of law, freedom of information and association and participation in government, as part of the matrix on country performance. In addition, good governance will be measured by a country's commitment to sound management of public expenditure programmes, greater accountability and the improvement of the legal and regulatory environment to encourage both public and private sector investment and, more particularly, in connection with performance in the following areas.

Accountability: The macro level includes financial accountability, in terms of an effective accounting system for expenditure control and cash management; and an external audit system. At the micro level, it requires accountability to the government of the managers of implementing agencies and parastatals for operations efficiency.

Transparency: Private sector investment decisions depend on public knowledge of the government's policies and confidence in its intentions, as well as information—in large part provided by the government—on economic and market conditions. Transparency of decisionmaking is also critical to the effectiveness of resource use and to the reduction of corruption and waste.

The Rule of Law: Predictable and stable legal and regulatory frameworks are essential for business to assess economic opportunities and act upon them without fear of arbitrary interference or expropriation. This requires that the rules be known in advance, that they actually be in force and be applied consistently and fairly; that conflicts be resolvable by an independent judicial system; and that procedures for amending and repealing the rules exist and be publicly known.

Participation: Good governance requires that directly and indirectly affected communities and groups should be able to participate in the design and implementation of programmes and projects. This aspect of governance is an essential element of securing commitment and support for projects and enhancing the quality of their implementation. Effective public participation depends on timely access to information about programmes and projects.

State Participants concluded that the Fund should play a role in supporting better governance through incorporating the aforementioned elements, where appropriate, into the substance of its dialogue with Fund borrowers, its economic and social reporting, and in the design of its operations.

18. Appropriate weights attached to these indicators will continue to be reviewed by Management. On the basis of these indicators Management will assess country performance and will submit to the Board of Directors its recommendations on performance classification and possible reclassification and, as appropriate, on any resulting reallocation of resources. It shall also present monthly a table highlighting, for each country, the initial allocation, the revised allocation, the total amounts allocated and the justification for significant changes in the programme.

19. A country which is assessed as a strong performer shall be eligible for an enhanced programme, allowing its indicative lending programme to be increased by a maximum of 50 percent. A country which is assessed as a weak performer shall have its indicative lending programme reduced by a maximum of 50 percent. Special attention will be given at the Mid-Term Review to these ceilings. A satisfactory performer shall be eligible for its indicative lending programme. In a country which does not, or ceases to, meet any of the accepted performance criteria, Fund assistance shall be confined to a core programme or to no programme at all, when conditions are such that no meaningful Fund activities can be envisaged.

20. The size of a core programme shall not exceed 20 percent of the indicative lending programme. Fund operations would be restricted to activities which can be implemented successfully even in the face of adverse economic circumstances and policies. The programme should be aimed at maintaining a dialogue and laying the basis for future economic progress by supporting activities—including those improving human resource capacities and environmental conditions which aim at creating favorable conditions for orderly resumption of operations in the country. (pp. 4–9)

Increased Participation in Project Design and Implementation by Affected People:

(iv) developing policies and projects with environmental implications within a meaningful consultation programme with affected groups and interested NGOs. (p. 12)

They encouraged the Fund to strengthen internal mechanisms such that project beneficiaries, notably women, can become more involved in the design and implementation of project activities. (p. 15)

Bank Actions to Support Microenterprises:

36. State Participants welcomed Management's initiative to increase support for microenterprises and decided that this should be started on a pilot programme with AfDF units of account (UA) 15 million. The adequacy of this amount will be examined at the Mid-Term Review. The initiative should be embedded in the overall poverty-reduction strategy of the Fund, and should especially be used as an instrument to generate income and employment for the poorest groups in society. In the programme, special attention should be paid to women entrepreneurs. The pilot project should be carried out in selected countries with an enabling environment, whereby the selection should be based on the receptiveness for this initiative of the socio-political system, of the entrepreneurs and the banking system as well. The ultimate objective of this scheme should be to make its borrowers fit for and to widen their access to more formal credit delivery mechanisms, including those of commercial banks. Resources should be channeled through grassroots NGOs for the purpose of on lending to microentrepreneurs. Participating organizations should be carefully selected on the basis of their degree of professionality, their organizational capacity and their knowledge of and experience with lending activities. Loans to microenterprises should be based on sound accounting and banking principles. Management should present an elaborated proposal, including a clear-cut definition of the target group and guidelines on individual loans to microentrepreneurs, for approval to the Board of Directors. State participants further stressed that the Fund should assist in improving operational conditions facilitating the growth of microenterprises, and the development of the private sector, in general. They also called on the Fund to cooperate with other development institutions engaged in supporting microenterprises. (p. 14)

Evaluate Results of Technical Assistance:

State participants requested Fund Management to undertake a full evaluation of what has been achieved by TAF [Technical Assistance Fund] so far, and report the results of the study to the Board of Directors and State Participants at the time of the Mid-Term Review. (p. 17)

Efforts to Improve the Quality of Project Development and Implementation:

44. State Participants welcomed the Report of the Task Force on Project Quality. They also took note of Management's comprehensive review of the Action Plan earlier approved by the Board. They urged Management to sustain the momentum of time-bound and monitorable measures to implement the key recommendations in the Report of the Task Force, including but not limited to, the following:

(i)   addressing the problems of design and loan conditionality relating to economic and pricing criteria; and strengthening the quality of appraisals and environmental documentation of projects;

(ii)   supervising all projects, and increasing significantly the number and size of supervision missions;

(iii)   instituting mid-term project evaluations and reformulating projects, if necessary;

(iv)   strengthening oversight of the procurement process, including adopting standard bidding documents and submitting procurement disbursements annually to the Board of Directors;

(v)   strengthening donor coordination and programme design within an overall country framework;

(vi)   strengthening the Operations Evaluation Office;

(vii)   undertaking annual country portfolio reviews;

(viii) ensuring that the design of all new projects incorporate lessons learned from country and/or sector experience; and

(ix)   CSPs [Country Strategy Papers] should play a key role in improving loan quality and should serve as a reference document for developing projects. Each year, when the first project proposal for a country is submitted to the Board, an updated CSP should be discussed by the Board prior to the project. Such an updated CSP should reflect, among other things: lending strategy and priorities; the results of the annual country portfolio review; donor coordination; activities undertaken to improve loan design; discussions with the country's authorities with regard to creating a sound overall policy environment; and the results and conclusions of Project Completion Reports (PCRs) and Project Performance Audit Reports (PPARs).

The implementation of these and other related measures will be monitored regularly by Management and reported to the Board of Directors. This will be a subject of a thorough examination at the time of the Mid-Term Review. (pp. 17–18)

Need for Independent Audit Function:

52. The Fund should maintain a strong and independent internal audit function. Its mandate should be extended to include the examination of operational and financial procedures and practices. It should report directly to the President and the Board of Directors. (p. 21)

Note: In addition to material on how replenishment resources will be used, similar to that normally contained in all MDB replenishment agreements, this agreement explicitly ties through tranches donor payments of replenishment resources to the achievement of certain objectives as specified below:

…the first tranche conditions would be the same as those for concluding ADF-VII consultations and bringing the replenishment into effect; the second tranche would be conditioned on the progress made in the implementation of institutional reforms, including the approval, by the Board of Directors, of a time-bound and monitorable Action Plan for both the Special Study on Governance and Related Matters and the Special Review of Certain Aspects of the Bank's Policies and Operations, and the rigorous implementation of the credit and loan cancellation policies. The third tranche would depend on the satisfactory outcome of the Mid-Term Review by the State Participants and progress in implementing the key recommendations from the Special Study on Governance and Related Matters and the Special Review of Certain Aspects of the Bank's Policies and Operations. (p. 23)

58. On the basis of Management reports, the review should consider the progress made in implementing the decisions set out in this Report, and particularly:

(ii)   The experience of the system of performance-based allocation and the adequacy of the ceilings noted in para 19;

(iv)   The progress made in defining and implementing the new directions on support to microenterprises and the adequacy of the amount allocated to the pilot programme;

(v)   The experience of policy-based lending, including a rigorous analysis of compliance with conditionality;

(vi)   The full evaluation of TAF operations asked for in paragraph 41;

(vii)   The progress made on the loan quality issues mentioned in paragraphs 43–47;

(viii)   The progress made in implementing the procurement oversight and reporting mentioned in para 44(iv);

(ix)   The progress made on the organizational, management and staffing issues mentioned in paragraphs 48 to 52;

This mid-term review will form the basis of the release of the third commitment tranche. In this context, the following criteria will have to be assessed positively:

—   implementation of a loan cancellation policy and annual portfolio reviews;

—   significant improvement in the ratio of operational to administrative costs;

—   implementation of regular supervision missions; 1–2 missions annually for each project. Management to examine financial repercussions of increased supervision missions. (p. 24)

Background Papers Prepared for the Task Force[72]

Nancy Alexander
The World Bank's Loan Portfolio Management: How Reforms Can Reduce Poverty

> Ms. Alexander is the project manager for the Development Bank Watchers' Project at the Bread for the World Institute. This is a large multiyear project funded by a number of major U.S. foundations. Prior to this she worked as the institute's director for domestic and international advocacy on issues relating to poverty and hunger. She has previously designed and facilitated energy and environment projects. She also worked as a legislative advocate for the Friends Committee on National Legislation.

Doug Bandow
Policy Reform: Necessary for Economic Growth and Poverty Reduction

> Mr. Bandow is a nationally syndicated columnist whose work has appeared in the *New York Times*, the *Wall Street Journal*, and the *Washington Post*. A senior fellow at the CATO Institute, he is the author of *Tripwire: Korea and U.S. Foreign Policy in a Changed World*; *Perpetuating Poverty: The World Bank, the IMF, and the Developing World* (coeditor); and other works. He was the former editor of *Inquiry Magazine* and served as a special assistant to President Reagan.

David Bathrick
Agricultural Development for Global Well-Being: Expanded Roles for the MDBs

> Dr. Bathrick is currently a technical adviser at Chemonics International Inc., where he provides support to the firm's international agriculture, natural resource, and rural development activities. He has 25 years of frontline strategy development and management experience in Latin America, Asia, and Washington, D.C. He has done extensive work with multifaceted projects and programs directed toward poverty amelioration, sustainable agriculture, and food security concerns. He is past president of the Association for International Agricultural and Rural Development.

---

72. Papers prepared for the Task Force were used as background material and were not specifically reviewed or endorsed by the group. Opinions expressed in them should not be attributed to the Task Force or its members.

James Burnham
"Additionality" in Multilateral Development Bank Operations

>   Dr. Burnham is the Murrin Professor of Global Competitiveness at Duquesne University's School of Business. He has been staff director at the president's Council of Economic Advisers (1981–1982), U.S. executive director at the World Bank (1982–1985), and a staff member of the Federal Reserve Board in Washington, D.C. He has also served as financial economist, chair of the Country Review Committee, and senior vice president and manager of Global Treasury at Mellon Bank.

Jonathan Fox
Promoting Independent Assessments of MDB Poverty Reduction Investments: Bringing Civil Society In

>   Dr. Fox is an associate professor of social science at the University of California, Santa Cruz. He was an international affairs fellow at the Council on Foreign Relations (1995–1996). From 1988–1995 he held assistant and associate professor positions at the Massachusetts Institute of Technology. He is the author of numerous books and articles on international development aid, governance, and social movements in Latin America.

John Gershman
The MDBs and Poverty Reduction

>   Mr. Gershman is a research associate at the Institute for Development Research and the Institute for Health and Social Justice in Boston. He is a doctoral candidate in the Department of Political Science at the University of California, Berkeley. Previously, Mr. Gershman was the managing director of the Philippine Resource Center (1988–1990) and worked at the Institute for Food and Development Policy (1991–1995), first as a research associate and subsequently as the outreach director. He has coedited two books, *Trading Freedom: How Free Trade Affects Our Lives, Work, and Environment* and *Reexamining and Renewing the Philippine Progressive Vision.*

James Hass
Rethinking the Role of the MDBs in Privately Financed Infrastructure: The Case for a Fundamental Review

>   Mr. Hass serves as the managing director of Capital Advisors, a Washington, D.C.-based consulting firm. Mr. Hass has been an investment banker specializing in infrastructure finance, where he was one of the first to use credit insurance in the municipal bond market. He has also done contract work with the North American Development Bank and the Tiete Parana Development Agency in Brazil, and for the Inter-American Development Bank.

Marshall Kaplan
Whither or Whether the MDBs: The Future of Multilateral Development Banks
The MDBs and Evaluation: A U.S. Perspective

> Dr. Kaplan is dean and professor of public policy at the University of Colorado's Graduate School of Public Affairs. He also served as deputy assistant secretary at the Department of Housing and Urban Development (1977–1981). He has authored numerous books on urban policy, infrastructure finance, and access to capital for developing countries. He directed two major congressional studies on infrastructure finance and urban policy and poverty. Recently he coordinated a World Bank–supported series of policy papers on sovereign and country risk, risk allocation, housing finance, and privatization in Mexico.

James Kunder
A Strategic Priority for the MDBs: Full Partnership with the Private Nonprofits

> Mr. Kunder was the vice president for program development at the Save the Children Federation. He has also served as the chair of the International Working Group on Armed Conflict and Displacement and as director of the U.S. Agency for International Development's Office of Foreign Disaster Assistance and is a former vice president of a private health care organization in the United States. He has worked for members of both the House of Representatives and the Senate.

Stephen Lande
The Impact of MDB Programs on a Number of U.S. Commercial Interests

> Mr. Lande is the President of Manchester Trade Ltd. and an adjunct professor of international trade at Georgetown University. Mr. Lande served as the First Assistant U.S. Trade Representative, in which capacity he established the USTR's bilateral relations section and led U.S. negotiating teams, including those for automotive trade with Japan, Mexico's accession to the General Agreement on Tariffs and Trade (GATT), and numerous other high-level negotiations.

John Mullen
Private Sector Development and Poverty Reduction: Are They Linked?

> Mr. Mullen previously served as president/CEO of the Romanian-American Enterprise Fund. He also served as the U.S. Agency for International Development's deputy general counsel, acting general counsel, deputy assistant administrator for democracy and governance, and assistant administrator for private enterprise. He was also a special assistant to Secretary of State Lawrence Eagleburger. His areas of expertise include project finance, privatization, capital markets development, and venture capital.

Arnold Nachmanoff
Rethinking the Role of the MDBs in Privately Financed Infrastructure: The Case for a Fundamental Review

> Mr. Nachmanoff is managing director at Capital Advisors, Ltd. and president of Nachmanoff Associates, Ltd. From 1977–1981 he was deputy assistant secretary of the Treasury in charge of the multilateral development banks. He has also served as financial adviser to various developing-country governments and has extensive private-sector experience. He recently served as principal adviser to the IDB's High Level Group on Private Sector Development.

Paul Nelson
The Multilateral Development Banks and Rapid Sustained Poverty Reduction: Progress, Limitations, and Recommendations

> Mr. Nelson is visiting research scholar at the University of Maryland's Government and Politics Department, where he is researching the transnational network of NGOs, factors involved in implementing policy change at the World Bank, and the role of official aid donors in directing economic and political development. He is author of *The World Bank and Non-Governmental Organizations: The Limits of Apolitical Development* (1995). He also served as associate director for development policy at Church World Services and Lutheran World Relief.

Lucy P. Nichols
Multilateral Debt: Dimensions of the Problem and Implications

> Ms. Nichols is a lecturer at the Institute for Development Studies at the University of Sussex and at the Harvard Institute for International Development. She has been a consultant to the Secretariat for the World Bank-IMF Development Committee Task Force on the Multilateral Development Banks, to the Bretton Woods Institution, and to the Inter-American Development Bank. Ms. Nichols assisted Tony Killick of the Overseas Development Institute (London) in preparing "Adjustment with Growth: Some Unsettled Questions," a paper for the Group of 24.

Patti L. Petesch
Profile of Global Poverty
Targeting the Poor: Survey of Donor Assessments of MDB Effectiveness

> Ms. Petesch is currently a consultant in international development whose clients include the World Bank, the Bread for the World Institute, and the Friedrich Ebert Foundation. Previously, she was a staff associate in the Poverty and Environment Program at the Overseas Development Council. Ms. Petesch is coauthor of *Sustaining the Earth: Role of Multilateral Development Institutions.*

Kevin F. F. Quigley
Prospects for Partnerships Between Foundations and MDBs

Dr. Quigley is the vice president for contemporary affairs and corporate programs at the Asia Society. He was a guest scholar at the Woodrow Wilson Center for International Scholars, where he directed a project looking at the efforts
to promote democracy in central Europe. Formerly, he served as director of
public policy at the Pew Charitable Trusts. He was a resident associate at the
Carnegie Endowment for International Peace. Dr. Quigley also served as the
legislative director for Senator John Heinz and as a budget examiner at the
Office of Management and Budget.

Gustav Ranis
On Fast-Disbursing Policy-Based Loans

Dr. Ranis is the director of the Yale Center of International and Area Studies
and the Frank Altschul Professor of International Economics at Yale University. He previously served as the U.S. Agency for International Development's
assistant administrator for programs and policy, and as a consultant to the
World Bank, the ADB, the UN Development Program, and the Ford and Rockefeller Foundations. Dr. Ranis has published extensively on various development issues, including *The Political Economy of Development Policy Change*
(1992) and *En Route to Modern Economic Growth: Latin America in the 1990s*
(1994).

Musunuru S. Rao
MDBs' Poverty Reduction Efforts, Experience, and Prospects

Dr. Rao served in the Asian Development Bank as manager of the Social
Development Division and various agricultural divisions. He also served as act-
ing director of the Social Sciences and Human Resources Division at the International Development Research Center (IDRC) in Canada. Prior to this, he was
a research analyst at the Rockefeller and Ford Foundations in New Delhi. He
has also published and prepared papers on development issues, including
women in development, poverty reduction, social development, and policy and
strategy formulation.

T. N. Srinivasan
Development Experience: Hong Kong and India 1960–1995

Dr. Srinivasan is the Samuel C. Park, Jr. Professor of Economics and director of
the Economic Growth Center at Yale University. He was a professor at the
Indian Statistical Institute in Delhi (1964–1977) and has taught at the University of Minnesota, the Massachusetts Institute of Technology, Johns Hopkins
University, and Stanford University. At the World Bank, Dr. Srinivasan served
as a special adviser to the Development Research Center (1977–1980) and as a
member of the editorial board of the *World Bank Review* (1986–1991). He has

published extensively on international trade, development, agricultural economics, and microeconomic theory.

J. D. Von Pischke
Risk, Reporting, and Relevance in World Bank Credit Projects

Dr. Von Pischke is an international consultant specializing in agricultural finance, microenterprise finance, credit policy, and other related topics. His assignments have included work for the World Bank, IFAD, the U.S. Agency for International Development, and several African countries. Formerly, he served as director of the Financial Sector Development Project Phase II at the Barents Group and as a senior financial analyst at the World Bank in a number of different departments. Dr. Von Pischke has published extensively on numerous development issues, including *Small Firms Informally Financed: Studies from Bangladesh* (1994).

Lawrence Yanovitch
The Multilateral Development Banks and the Microfinance Sector: An Introduction to the Issues

Mr. Yanovitch is a specialist in microenterprise and currently serves as the director of policy and research at the Foundation for International Community Assistance (FINCA). He has field experience in Latin America, Africa, Asia, the former Soviet states, and the United States. Several recent projects include managing the Latin America/Africa Guarantee Facility and the Regional Village Banking Initiative in Central America and East Africa. Mr. Yanovitch is also the cochair of the Microenterprise Coalition and a member of the Policy Advisory Group for the World Bank Microfinance Consultative Group.

Additional Statements of Task Force Members

George B. N. Ayittey

Distinction between "Crisis" and "Lack of Development"

An understanding of Africa's woes necessitates a distinction between "crisis" and "underdevelopment." Because their causes are different, solutions prescribed for one may not be suitable for the other. By definition, a crisis is a serious adverse condition that requires immediate attention. There is an element of urgency. A crisis cannot persist for long without a major social upheaval or economic explosion. Perhaps an analogy would be appropriate here.

Consider the development process as embarking on a journey in a *vehicle*, leaving Point A (state of underdevelopment) and going to Point B (developed state). The road is strewn with "obstacles." In the development literature, a host of "obstacles" were identified: poverty, low investment, low savings, illiteracy, high population growth rates, etc. The interplay of these factors produced the notorious "vicious cycle of poverty."

The "vehicle" for this journey may be private or state-owned. In virtually all African countries, a STATE vehicle (statism) was chosen after independence and one man claimed the divine right to be the driver for life ("president for life"). But this state vehicle is in terrible shape: no brakes or shock absorbers (no checks and balances). The fan belt is ripped, which means its cooling system is inoperative. Drive the vehicle three or four miles and it will overheat (inflation). The vehicle is overloaded, with members of the president's tribe sitting in the front seats. One of its tires is flat and consequently the ride is likely to be bumpy. A goat has been tied to the rear bumper.

Somewhere along the way, the smoke-belching, dilapidated vehicle has broken down: dead battery, radiator overheated with the coolant boiling over. This is a "crisis" situation that must be resolved *before* continuing on the journey. Removing obstacles on the road (building schools to improve literacy rates or sinking boreholes for drinking water) would not make any difference to the journey (development). This vehicle is going nowhere fast. Changing the driver through democratic elections or coups d'état would not make any difference either.

Therefore the questions of "poverty reduction," "accelerating," or "promoting environmentally sustainable" development (getting to Point B faster) must be deferred for now *until the vehicle is fixed* (reformed). That requires an understanding of the cause of the vehicle breakdown (hence, the African crisis).

The vehicle is composed of two defective systems: statism and sultanism (personal or one-man rule). By statism is meant state hegemony in the economy and the direction of economic activity or development by the state through such devices as price controls, legislative acts, regulations and state ownership of the means of production and operation of state enterprises. Personal rule is the monopolization of political power by one individual, the grotesque forms being "president for life" and military dictatorship. Opposition parties were outlawed and countries were declared "one-party states" in the postcolonial era.

These monstrous systems were characterized by a great deal of concentration of power in the hands of the state and, ultimately, one individual. This transformed the state into something like a pot of gold, which all sorts of individuals and groups competed to capture—competition that often degenerated into civil war: Angola, Mozambique, etc. Once captured, the state machinery was used by the head of state to advance the economic interests of himself (kleptocracy), his cronies (cronyism), relatives (nepotism), and tribesmen (tribalism). All others were EXCLUDED—the politics of exclusion. Those excluded from the good life had two options available to them: Either rise up to overthrow the ruling elites and replace them with themselves, or secede (e.g., Biafra in 1967, Somaliland Republic in 1993 [*sic*]). Either prospect resulted in violence, carnage, and chaos.

Concept of "Government" in Africa

"Government" as it is known in the United States does not exist in many parts of Africa. What exists in Africa is a "MAFIA" or "VAMPIRE STATE"—that is, a state hijacked by a coterie of con artists, gangsters, and crooks to enrich themselves. The richest persons in Africa are heads of state and ministers. "Government" is not a vehicle to serve but to fleece the people, through confiscatory taxes, levies, and other state controls.

Are the bandits "committed" to poverty reduction? Of course! Reducing *their* own poverty! Would they implement reforms? As I described in a July 1996 *Wall Street Journal* editorial, "If pressured, they would only adopt those cosmetic 'reforms' that ensure continued flow of Western aid. But most Africans dismiss this reform posturing as the 'Babangida boogie': one step forward, three steps back, a sidekick and flip to land on a fat Swiss bank account." The Kenyan version of this ritual dance, the Moi massamba, was well described by the *Economist* (August 19, 1995):

Over the past few years, Kenya has performed a curious mating ritual with its aid donors. The steps are: One, Kenya wins its yearly pledges for foreign aid. Two, the government begins to misbehave, backtracking on economic reform and behaving in an authoritarian manner. Three, a new meeting of donor countries looms with exasperated foreign governments preparing their sharp rebukes. Four, Kenya pulls a placatory rabbit out of the hat. Five, the donors are mollified and the aid is pledged. The whole dance then starts again. (p. 37)

How do the MDBs deal with such "gangster regimes"? Keep in mind that, under international law, the people of a country cannot be held liable for a loan to an illegitimate regime, contracted without their express approval. Furthermore,

Task Force recommendations of MDBs' active support for improved governance with focus on rule of law, respect for property rights, containment of corruption are all in the right direction. "Taking a more proactive stance on governance," however, will clash with the issue of sovereignty—"meddling in internal affairs of a developing country," a charge that is constantly hurled by Third World despots to block reform.

Proposals

There are two ways to tackle this problem:

Create/support local watchdogs. This charge can be *evaded* if local watchdog groups could be encouraged to do what you have recommended for the MDBs: ensuring rule of law, property rights, empowering the poor, etc. This has another important implication as well. Reform that is *internally generated* is far more sustainable than that which is externally "imposed" or "dictated." Keep in mind that, ultimately, it is Africans who must solve their own problems. Internally generated reforms also provide "ownership"—"Ghana-made" reforms—and there is always "pride of ownership."

On page 43, the Task Force report remarked that "The MDBs should [approve lending only when] reforms are strongly supported and 'owned' by the local government." "Ownership" must appropriately be applied to the *people*, not the local "mafia" government.

Also keep in mind that most of your recommendations regarding "governance" are not new or unknown to the local NGOs. They are just powerless or afraid to advocate them. As a result, there is no *internal* pressure to reform, only the external—from the MDBs. Our recommendations should be such as to strengthen and unleash the internal agents of reform and watchdogs, independent press and public-policy think tanks or development-oriented NGOs, run by private citizens.

Some funding support should be made available to them. Recall the success of Solidarity—an independent trade union—in Poland. These local organizations can be more critical than the MDBs in their assessment of governance. As you stated, "The MDBs have been constrained in their response to these problems by occasional overly restrictive interpretations of their articles of agreement against consideration of noneconomic factors in their activities and by the reluctance of some of their executive directors to support a more active position on governance concerns." (page 40) LET THE LOCAL WATCHDOGS DO IT AND SUPPORT THEM IN THIS EFFORT! If any local NGO funded by the MDBs is shut down, the errant government risks losing access to MDB credit.

Alternative eligibility requirements. Please keep in mind that eligibility criteria that are too broad and somewhat nebulous would be difficult to apply or achieve. I can identify about seven elements of the criteria you have proposed: from accountability, rule of law, minimizing corruption, transparency to low-priority uses of scarce resources. I think it would be useful to focus like a hawk on a few key institutions that would allow you the *same* goals. These institutions, in my view, are

❏ an independent central bank,

❏ an independent judiciary, and

❏ an independent press/media.

If Africa had just these three, I assure you that about 70 percent of the continent's problems would be resolved.

Index of Economic Freedom

On page 37, the Task Force report noted:

> On the basis of numerous studies and much past experience, the Task Force believes that the MDBs should only conduct lending operations in countries that are maintaining a policy framework adequate to permit economically, environmentally, and socially sustainable growth.... Obviously, it is impossible to formulate universally applicable specific criteria for policy adequacy in each of these areas, but the following are the kinds of issues to be examined:
>
> • Economic policies—substantial freedom from restriction on prices and production, adequate fiscal and monetary policies, policies needed for domestic and foreign investment, policies that safeguard property rights, and the limitation of the public sector to appropriate activities only.

I would like to draw your attention to the fact that an attempt has been made to formulate one such universally applicable criterion and that's the Index of Economic Freedom. The Heritage Foundation of Washington, D.C., and The Fraser Institute of Vancouver, Canada, attempted to find the correlation between economic freedom and wealth around the world over a 20-year period.

> Stripped to its essentials, economic freedom is concerned with property rights and choice. Individuals are economically free if property that they have legally acquired is protected from invasions or intrusions by others, and if they are free to use, exchange or give away their property so long as their actions do not violate other people's similar rights. That sounds abstract but it comes to life as soon as you think of how a government might restrict this freedom. Failing to protect property rights would be one way. Others would be to confiscate property, to require individuals to give up their time through military conscription, to lay down rules for what they may buy or sell and at what price. A more subtle, but just as destructive, way would be to pursue monetary policies that lead to hyperinflation, eroding the value of money. (*Economist*, January 13, 1996, p. 21)

In terms of broad geographic regions, the study found that "apart from a handful of Middle Eastern countries, sub-Saharan Africa was the only area of the world that enjoyed no appreciable improvement in its level of economic freedom between 1975–1995."[73]

Individual African countries may be placed in three categories:[74]

Borderline (Score: 5.0)	**Mostly Free** (Score: 5.0–4.0)	**Repressed** (Score: under 4.0)
Botswana	South Africa	Madagascar
	Ghana	Benin
	Gabon	Egypt
	Kenya	Nigeria
	Mali	Morocco
	Malawi	Rwanda
	Tunisia	Uganda
	Sierra Leone	Tanzania
	Cameroon	Togo
	Central African Republic	Niger
	Senegal	Zambia
		Congo
		Zimbabwe
		Burundi
		Côte d'Ivoire
		Algeria
		Zaire

Recommendation

MDB lending should automatically be CUT OFF to any country where, over a five-year period,

❐   its index of economic freedom does not improve by one point,

❐   its budget deficits continuously exceed 10 percent of GDP every year, and

❐   the annual increase in the money supply exceeds 15 percent consecutively.

---

73. Their findings are reported in the *Economist*, January 13, 1996, p. 21. This is also cited by Nicholas Eberstadt in the *Washington Times*, October 7, 1996, p. A19.

74. Compiled from the *Economist*, January 13, 1996, p. 22.

Barbara Bramble

As a member of the CSIS Task Force on the question of the United States and Multilateral Development Banks, I am submitting this separate opinion on the questions presented to the members for a vote, concerning the role of the MDBs in private-sector funding.

1.   The first issue is presented by Options Concerning Extent and Nature of Direct MDB Support for Private Projects, beginning on page 49. In my view these options are not clearly differentiated, or not differentiated along the appropriate lines. For example, Option 4 is a confusing combination of both increasing the *time period* of the programs and the *amount of resources* devoted to them. These should be separate options. Option 3 would keep the programs modest in size but cut them off too quickly.

So I am recommending an additional option, which I think several members of the Task Force might have selected if it had been offered. A combination of Option 3 and Option 4, it would keep the programs more or less at current levels, as in Option 3, but allow them to continue for a longer time (though still with a defined end point), as in Option 4.

The reason this is important is hinted at in Option 4, "it is in everyone's interest to allow a somewhat longer time period before the MDBs cease providing limited support to private projects...so that reforms are solidified and reversals...are avoided." The key role for the MDBs in supporting private projects may not be in their financing at all, but in the Strengthened Conditions that form the first section of both Options 3 and 4. The Task Force insists there should be a Framework Agreement with the country where the project will be located as a precondition for private-sector lending. This Agreement would call for new policies in economics and investment, public policy (which should include a whole range of social issues as called for in the Action Plan from the Copenhagen Summit on Social Development, in addition to the environment, which is mentioned in the text), and specific sectors. But these new policies may need years to be implemented, and to become normal operating procedure, for example, in the areas of efficient regulatory systems, monitoring, and law enforcement. The MDBs can play a constructive role in economic and policy analysis, advice, finding resources for capacity-building, convening the relevant players for decision making, etc. They are more likely to do so if they are financially involved, if even in a minor way. Clear graduation benchmarks would be negotiated with each country as part of the Framework Agreement.

If these private investments are useful for long-term development at all, as they are often justified, it may well be because they are associated with the new policies of the Framework Agreements. And the Agreements must be supported for some years to ensure change that will last.

2.   Focus of Responsibility for Private-Sector Transactions. Here too the options are not clearly differentiated. The consolidation of all responsibility for private-sector transactions in IFC should not take place until it is clear that IFC will apply the same procedures and policies, on environmental and social issues, as the other members of the World Bank Group. This is sometimes called "upward harmonization." Thus selection of the first option under Recommendation 6c

(consolidation of responsibility in IFC) should mean *only after, or if, such harmonization has taken place*. But this option was not offered.

On the other hand, this could be just as delayed as the attempt to change the IBRD charter to remove the requirement for a government guarantee. Thus, the idea of sequential changes, as described in the paragraph following Recommendation 6c on page 52, is meaningless.

Because both options imply delays, in a choice between the options that were offered, I would vote for the second option under Recommendation 6c (consolidation within the main World Bank). This would ensure a closer coordination of policy under one roof than does the present situation of separate, but not really separate, institutions. But if a third option of consolidation within IFC, after upward harmonization, were available, that would be acceptable too, and perhaps it would come about earlier.

Nancy Alexander joins in this separate opinion.

Robert S. Browne

The "Washington Consensus" (the reforms repeatedly referred to in the document) is not fully accepted as valid policy by all the relevant actors. Many Africans articulate strong opposition to the requirement that they liberalize their trade regimes, thereby opening their economies to the risk of immediate deindustrialization of their nascent, if small, industrial sectors.

An alternative that they propose is the supporting of integrated subregional economic entities, which would maintain trade barriers against foreign consumer goods that the Africans hoped to produce for themselves, while allowing free trade within the subregional entity. Such trade restriction would buy them a window of opportunity in which to develop the skills to become internationally competitive, at which time they could more safely liberalize their trade regimes with the outside world. The MDBs could offer myriad types of support to these subregional entities. To the extent that this report recommends trade liberalization as a precondition for MDB financing, I must withhold my support for such a requirement.

I would also call attention to the informal "burden-sharing" agreements among the major MDB donor countries, which informally link the size of other donors' contributions to the size of the United States' paid-in contribution. It is entirely inappropriate for the United States to terminate, unilaterally, its financial contribution to these international organizations in view of this linkage, rather than negotiate the matter with the other major donors.

James B. Burnham

I am in substantial agreement with most of the Task Force's recommendations for improvement in the operations of the multilateral development banks. However, with respect to U.S. financial support, my strong preference for the "no further new contributions" option needs a word of elaboration, because the reasoning for this choice is not fully developed.

In advocating "no new contributions," one can continue to support, as I do, a useful—if less ambitious—role for the MDBs. The report amply demonstrates that the underlying raison d'être for these institutions—a poorly functioning international capital market—is rapidly losing its persuasiveness. Although it is in U.S. interests to have at least one technically competent, moderately financed multilateral organization focusing on international development, the report does not make a case for the scale and scope of the existing set of institutions.

Support of "no new contributions" also rests heavily on the fact that nearly all MDBs can rely on already agreed capital contributions and internal resources (e.g., retained earnings) for continuing high—and expanding—levels of activity. For example, the World Bank in 1996 received over $12 billion in loan repayments, which can be recycled to new borrowers. The Bank has calculated that in 1996, its loans outstanding were only 55 percent of its Statutory Lending Limit of over $200 billion, which can be increased every year through its own considerable earnings. The "soft" loan windows of the MDBs enjoy increasing repayments—over $500 million annually in the case of IDA, in addition to the grants that it receives from the World Bank.

By stressing "no new contributions" (beyond those formal funding commitments already made by executive agreement and congressional authorization), the report's praiseworthy objective of refocusing the activities of the MDBs can be more easily achieved. This would be particularly true if the Secretary of the Treasury were willing to work to persuade his G-7 colleagues to adopt a similar course of action.

Irvin D. Coker

I believe that far too often, there is still not enough consideration given to lessons learned or piloting activities to ascertain whether something is workable. The development specialists, development economists, and others knowledgeable about economic growth believe that insufficient resources are provided for micro, small, and medium-scale enterprises to aid in the overall economic growth of a nation. The MDBs' resources could go far in assisting nations with reasonable development policies and good democracy and governance to invest more in private-sector development. Without a doubt, investment in microenterprise does go a long way in lifting many out of poverty, even though, in my opinion, not enough employment opportunities are generated to reduce unemployment significantly. The means of measuring the parameters of microenterprise, even though not mentioned in the paper, could be expanded to permit the generation of employment opportunities beyond the proprietary family or household unit to have significant impact on the unemployed.

Insufficient attention is given to the effective use of local experts and consultants in many of the MDBs' projects. There are too many instances of bank staff seeking employment opportunities for the bank's retired staff or colleagues from selected geographic areas outside of the beneficiary country. This biased approach gets, at times, a level of energy by the bank's staff that causes serious concerns for the borrowing-country officials, who shy away from challenging these appearances of unethical behavior. This type of questionable selection is done at the expense of local experts and fair competitive process of experts from the United States and other countries.

Another issue is the desire to seek the services of only large firms for implementation of projects as the only insurance to get the job done "right." Quality is not necessarily the measuring factor, but cost and the level of expenditure of resources take precedence over the condition of the final product. The actions of bank staff create accountability and implementation problems that add to the poor state of success of these activities. The lack of on-the-ground staff also adds to the questionable quality of projects and possibly excessive cost versus planned expenditure levels. The parachuting of experts in and out on an infrequent basis does not ensure better monitoring or timely decision making about implementation issues.

Catherine Gwin

Although there are many points within the CSIS Task Force report on the U.S. interests and the MDBs with which I strongly agree, there is much I find seriously problematic.

Among the major points with which I agree are the following:

❑ The MDBs' objectives of reducing poverty and promoting broad-based, environmentally sustainable growth remain important to U.S. interests.

❑ MDBs have important strengths. They also have weaknesses, many of which are caused by policies and pressures of their shareholders, and should be the continuing source of attention and reform. Most important is the need for stricter adherence to performance-based lending by all MDBs. In this regard, the report is right to urge that MDB lending be supportive of good performers.

❑ MDBs should do more to take account of increasing access to private capital by their traditional borrowers. In particular, there is much that the MDBs can do to help countries create a conducive environment for private-sector investment (both domestic and international).

❑ MDBs should continue to increase their transparency and accountability and, where now weak, improve their project and program evaluation.

None of these points are new points, however; and the report does too little to distinguish where they are and where they are not being dealt with by the different institutions.

Where I take further serious issue with the report is on the following points:

❑ The report fails to distinguish appropriately among the MDBs, making statements of both praise and criticism as if they applied equally across the different institutions.

❏ For the most part, it misdefines the key issues regarding the MDBs' role in the area of private-sector development. This was an issue comprehensively laid out in a 1995 Overseas Development Council publication, *Moving to the Market: The World Bank in Transition*, by Richard Richardson and Jonas Haralz. I will not try to summarize that study here, but only repeat two points. One, there are good reasons and good opportunities for the MDBs, particularly the World Bank Group, to influence both the direction and the character of private enterprise financing in the developing world. However, amending the IBRD's articles to dispense with its sovereign guarantee requirement so as to undertake nonrecourse financing to private enterprises, as the Task Force report raises, is not likely to be the most efficacious way to strengthen the Bank's support for private-sector development. Two, making a choice between the Bank or IFC as the principal mechanism for the World Bank Group's involvement on these issues, as the Task Force report would have us do, is a false choice because the two have very different, and presumably complementary, roles to play.

❏ The report's statement about U.S. interests and recommendations on a funding strategy are inconsistent. The interests as stated justify a more unequivocal stand on making up arrears and then determining future funding "needs" on the basis of the institutions' and their borrowers' performance.

❏ Throughout, the report fails to make adequate distinctions between hard and soft loan windows; and the differing capacities and needs of the non-concessional and concessional borrowers. Both windows should be more strictly performance-based; but the MDBs need to play different roles in different categories of countries.

❏ As noted above, although the report repeats a great deal of what has been said previously (and what amounts to existing U.S. policy), it fails to distinguish what is and what is not being done.

❏ Furthermore, it recommends a kind of policy approach that continues to "move the goalpost" in a context in which U.S. benefits derive largely from the multilateral nature of the institutions.

I am aware that you and your colleagues at CSIS made a major effort to reach out to diverse views and expertise in preparing this report. I commend you for that; but I regret that the report does not fully represent the kind of positive, hard-hitting, and forward-looking policy statement that I would like to see the United States follow.

Representative Tony P. Hall

I am pleased to lend my support and endorsement to the findings of this ambitious and timely review of U.S. participation in the MDBs. The Center for Strategic and International Studies (CSIS) and the Ford Foundation are to be commended for this rigorous undertaking, and in particular for the participatory and inclusive manner in which the study was conducted. The end result reflects an emerging U.S. consensus on future directions for continued reform of the banks.

Under President Wolfensohn's adept and dedicated leadership, the Bank Group has embarked on a new reform initiative aimed at increasing the Bank's effectiveness in achieving its basic mission of reducing poverty. The findings and recommendations of this report offer a valuable contribution to the current reform process at the Bank Group. As such, I urge my colleagues serving on the relevant congressional committees, and those responsible for guiding the ongoing reform process at the Bank Group to give the report the thorough attention and consideration it deserves.

Now more than ever, as the wealthiest nation on Earth and as a world leader, the United States has much at stake in the success or failure of multilateral banks in combating poverty, and especially the cruelest forms of absolute poverty: *hunger and malnutrition*. Our well-being and that of our children greatly depends on what we do to foster global economic prosperity and stability—goals that will remain elusive in a world where 800 million people do not have enough to eat, and one-fifth of humanity struggles to survive on less than a dollar a day.

The Bank Group bears special responsibility to see that our investments are paying off in terms of real progress in reducing mass poverty and ensuring that economic growth policies and projects do not leave the poor behind. I believe that under Mr. Wolfensohn's unique guidance and vision, the Bank Group is beginning to make some steps in the right direction.

Yet, in weighing my endorsement of these recommendations for further reform, I cannot help but recall the Banks' earlier commitments to fighting hunger as an explicit goal and purpose of the institutions. I am endorsing these recommendations to the extent that, if adopted, they can contribute toward strengthening the banks' effectiveness in fighting hunger. However, much more remains to be done if the Bank Group is to meet its commitment to fighting hunger and malnutrition as priority objectives in the short and long run.

First, as the reform process moves forward, I would like to see the Bank Group give serious thought to what it can do to focus more direct and concerted attention on hunger and food security issues. Without an explicit focus within the Bank Groups' structure on hunger issues, will the Bank effectively collaborate in joint food security assessments and monitoring efforts with host governments, UN agencies, bilateral donors, and local and international nongovernmental organizations? Will it ensure that Bank policies and programs directly support and contribute to jointly defined national food security action plans? Will it ensure that the Banks' programs complement and strengthen local nongovernmental initiatives to reduce hunger, in the short run, among the most vulnerable?

Certainly, the Bank has contributed to gains some countries have made in overcoming hunger, and steps in the right direction have included the creation of the Consultative Group to Assist the Poorest (CGAP). However, I am concerned that with hunger-related issues parceled out among various networks and sectoral divisions at the Bank Group (agriculture, nutrition, social safety nets, rural development, social development, and poverty programs), efforts to coordinate antihunger programming and measure impact will be weak at best. Our own experience in the Congress shows the difficulties inherent in maintaining an effective focus on hunger issues let alone developing coherent antihunger policy when there is no institutional focal point for the issue, and it is instead fractured and diluted among several committees of jurisdiction

Second, the Bank Group should ensure that its programs of assistance contribute—or at the very least are not at odds with—national action plans on food security. This means that in developing country assistance strategies, the Bank Group must be willing and able to tackle politically sensitive equity issues that very often are basic root causes of poverty and hunger—namely, improved access to productive resources, such as land and credit, for the very poor. The Bank Group is to be applauded for recent attempts to more prominently feature social development issues in country strategies. However, this process needs to be accelerated, and equity considerations moved to the forefront of the planning process if real progress is to be made in overcoming hunger.

At the Bank's 1993 conference on "Overcoming Global Hunger," and more recently in the Bank's statement at the November 1996 World Food Summit, the Bank Group highlighted the multifaceted nature of hunger problems, and the need to attack it from various angles—technological, political, and economic. On these fronts and more, the Bank is already doing much to address hunger, and I believe such efforts will be enhanced by the recommendations of the Task Force's report. However, hunger issues tend to be obscured in the absence of an institutional mechanism to unify and coordinate antihunger policy among sectoral divisions within the Bank Group, and in the Bank Group's relationships with other antihunger players.

From a purely practical management perspective, a concerted focus on fighting hunger as a primary strategic goal for the Bank Group is imminently logical. Few would argue that there is any worse form of absolute poverty than the inability to obtain an adequate diet to live a healthy and productive life. In no other area would the Bank Group be in a better position to show compelling results or claim more direct and measurable impact in fulfilling its mandate of poverty alleviation than in reduced levels of malnutrition and improved food security.

As the Bank Group weighs the recommendations of this report, and as the Board of Governors prepares to convene its 1997 annual meeting, I would challenge the Bank Group to recommit itself to fighting hunger as a top institutional goal. Last fall, the Bank Group joined the majority of the world's nations in pledging to advance the World Food Summit goal of reducing by half the number of people facing hunger by the year 2015. To meet this commitment, it is time for the Bank Group to reassess its capacity to make measurable inroads in the fight against hunger, and ensure that further reforms support a renewed focus on this key issue of our time.

James Kunder

This report on the United States and the multilateral development banks is timely and useful. Let me suggest two ways it could have been even more valuable: by recognizing the implications of the "associational revolution" now under way around the world, and by emphasizing the human capital component of multilateral banking.

In its summary of the changed world we now face, the report mentioned (page 19) the expansion of nongovernmental entities. This "expansion" is, in fact, an explosion of voluntary associations—religious, secular, grassroots, international, technical, participatory—that is transforming, through the Internet and by knocking on doors, how human beings get things done in their communities. Much more could and should have been said in the report about how the MDBs can work creatively with this grassroots explosion to achieve mutual goals of development and human progress.

Similarly, this report touched on how investment in human capital—in education, health, drinking water, and sanitation—affects development, but missed an opportunity to push the MDBs beyond their traditional "bricks and mortar" orientation. Investment in basic education, for example, yields development returns as clear and measurable as investments in power plants—although not as compelling to certain categories of investors. In a mistaken rush to short-term "cost-effectiveness," MDB investments in human capital—like investments in corporate R&D—can be overlooked, with decidedly nonproductive long-term consequences. In its own development, the United States recognized the need to invest in public health and public schools as well as railroads and dams. It would have been appropriate in this report to recall the full range of investments necessary for progress.

Allan H. Meltzer

The Task Force report is a serious effort to reconcile the many divergent views expressed in Task Force meetings while retaining substance. The report makes many recommendations and observations that I share wholeheartedly. Examples include the following:

❐ The report recognizes that the role of the multilateral development banks (MDBs) has declined relatively and absolutely as capital markets have expanded to service developing and emerging countries. Much of the capital flows to a small subset of countries. One reason for this concentration is the absolute size of some developing countries. A more relevant measure, for many purposes, is the number of countries that now have access to the capital markets. This raises the issue of the MDBs' core competencies or competitive advantages that the report does not discuss.

❏ The report recommends terminating or phasing out some programs and expanding others such as microlending. In most cases, proposals for new programs are not based an any evidence that markets or local governments cannot or will not supply these services. Competitive advantage, core competency, or some other reason should be advanced to justify MDB programs.

❏ There is a good discussion of the reasons microenterprises have had problems in the past. There is also a good discussion of property rights in rural land, but there are no proposals to vest property rights.

❏ The report properly recognizes the poverty problem and acknowledges that years of MDB effort have made little difference. (The percentage living in poverty is approximately the same as 40 years ago; the absolute number has doubled.) The report calls for a higher level of commitment instead of opting for changes such as democratic government (in which the poor would be represented and their voices heard), property rights, and the rule of law. The report opts for subsidies and MDB programs instead of empowerment and ownership. Recommendation 8b does little more than exhort the MDBs to do better.

What Should Be Changed?

When the World Bank was established as one of the Bretton Woods institutions, the widespread belief was that, unless dramatic changes were made, the postwar political and economic order would replicate large parts of the interwar order. One of the Bank's tasks was to stimulate capital flows and overcome barriers to private lending from developed to emerging and developing nations.

The facts of postwar experience do not support this reasoning. Developing countries have had difficulty adjusting to too much lending, not too little. The debt crisis of the 1980s and Mexico's problems in the 1990s are examples. Moreover, countries that have opened their economies and embarked on promised reforms of budgets, regulations, and trade policies have had few difficulties entering the markets for debt, equity, or bank loans.

The report fails to explore the implications of this difference between early anticipations and experience in the past quarter century. It does not inquire whether annual lending at the level of the MDBs is desirable or useful. It does not ask whether U.S. policy should seek to restrict lending to those cases where private markets fail to support governments that open their markets and reform their economies.

Property Rights and the Rule of Law

The U.S. public supports the rule of law, property rights, personal freedom, and representative government. Where countries have moved toward these goals, opened their economies to trade and capital, and reduced regulation and state ownership, progress has followed. The report mentions several of these factors, some more than once. But it does not connect future U.S. support of the MDBs to these objectives. The report, therefore, misses the opportunity to redirect U.S. policy toward the MDBs in a way that is consistent with the public's widely shared objectives.

Redirection is in our interest and in the interest of the poorest countries. Introducing or greatly strengthening the rule of law, property rights, and political accountability reduces tyranny, corruption, and waste of resources on "prestige" projects and unnecessary military equipment.

U.S. policy should press the MDBs to demand sustained progress toward the rule of law, vested and secure property rights, and representative government.

Environment

The report makes repeated mention of "sustainable development" and protection of the environment. These terms, however, are never defined. No rational person would oppose steps toward environmental protection that raise living standards. No recognition is given to the trade-off between a better environment and a higher living standard that must often be made.

The proper trade-off for each country cannot be imposed from Washington or by MDBs. I believe that there is a minimum acceptable standard that should be established jointly with representative governments in the developing countries.

The minimum acceptable standard should be the basis for defining "sustainable development." The minimal acceptable standard should not be the same in countries heavily dependent on extractive industries as in countries with mainly light industry and tourist services. U.S. policy should encourage the establishment of regional and international tradable pollution permits to encourage economic growth while reducing pollution to the acceptable standard. This is a rational program for resolving conflicts between environmental and developmental concerns.

The report expresses concern about the "alarm" many people feel about the future environment. Such emotive reactions are a poor basis for policy and a poor reason for action. There are many unresolved cognitive and scientific issues about global warming and other environmental risks. These unresolved issues contribute to the difficulty of defining "sustainable development."

Interagency Duplication

The MDBs have overlapping responsibilities and, at times, duplication of effort. There are costs of duplication without the benefits of effective competition.

The report treats issues of organization and makes useful suggestions. But the report does not propose that individual MDBs develop separate areas of competence and excellence. If the MDBs do not specialize, there should be standards for comparing performance. These comparisons should affect funding.

Marginal Returns

The report sets out some of the experience in sustaining projects after MDB funding ends. The record is not good. Many projects terminate or deteriorate after funding stops.

Despite this poor record of sustaining objectives, the report (and the MDBs) greatly overstate their achievements. The reason is that often the most promising projects are presented for funding at the MDBs. Some of these projects would have high priority, so they are not on the margin.

Because funding can be transferred, within limits, between programs and projects, the marginal project funded by the MDBs often differs from the projects in the application. The marginal projects may have lower success rates than the projects for which funds are granted. As a result, it is difficult to know within a wide range what the development banks achieve. It is less than they report.

Charges for Services

The MDBs provide consulting services to governments. Private consultants provide competing services. A major difference is that the private consultants charge for their service, and the MDBs do not. Why does this persist? Should the MDBs charge for their consulting services and meet a market test?

Moral Hazard

Loan guarantees are discussed beginning on page 47. Guarantees raise issues of moral hazard, in this case the hazard of encouraging the behavior that they wish to avoid. Is there reason to believe that loan guarantees will not subsidize risky behavior? Why not insist on political and economic reforms to reduce the risk of default?

Conclusion

I believe that the United States should take the lead to

❏   increase the role of capital markets,

❏   phase out the MDBs over time,

❏   provide incentives to improve performance and achievements,

❏   eliminate duplication by developing core competencies at the World Bank and the regional banks, and

❏   encourage representative governments, the rule of law, property rights, and open markets.

Nicholas Eberstadt asks to be associated with these comments.

Representative Constance Morella

I endorse the thrust of the recommendations but have not had the time to participate in a number of task force meetings or to study all the quite detailed material produced by the group. I continue to believe that the multilateral development banks have an extremely important role to play and that internal changes which will make clear their effectiveness to the American people are critical.

Frances Seymour

World Wildlife Fund agrees with the general thrust of the report's conclusions and recommendations, in particular that MDB objectives remain important U.S. interests, that access to MDB resources should be conditioned on the adequacy of policy frameworks and governance of borrowers, and that MDB support for private projects should be selectively undertaken to promote development objectives and should be in accordance with upwardly harmonized project standards. However, the report does not provide an adequate treatment of the MDBs' current performance or potential role in promoting environmentally sustainable development. WWF believes that U.S. leadership is necessary to ensure fulfillment of existing commitments to improve MDB environmental performance. More important, such leadership is crucial to achieving consensus among MDB shareholders regarding new mandates and partnerships through which MDBs can actively assist individual countries and the global community in moving toward environmentally sustainable development paths.

Ian Vasquez and Doug Bandow

The CSIS Task Force has grappled with many of the problems—ranging from poor project performance and outdated missions to lack of accountability and openness—that have plagued the multilateral development banks (MDBs). The tone of the report suggests members' cautiousness, rather than enthusiasm, about the ability of MDBs to accomplish effectively many of their ambitious and noteworthy goals. That is a welcome change from the usual deferential treatment that MDBs receive from Washington's foreign policy establishment, although it is probably an inevitable change, given the MDBs' own acknowledgments of troubled lending and the need for reform.

In particular, three broad themes in the report represent moves in the right direction. First is the recognition that lending will do little good, and will likely be counterproductive, if the overall policies of a country are inimical to growth. In general terms, economic progress requires a market-oriented policy environment. The MDBs often point that out themselves, but, as the report suggests, they often continue to lend to governments regardless of their economic policies.

Second, the report's calls for changes at the MDBs, accompanied by benchmarks that can be used to judge whether the recommendations have been implemented, reflect Task Force members' impatience with some MDBs' seemingly endless promises and reform initiatives. In other words, the lending agencies should not expect to survive forever even if they proclaim themselves advocates of reform. Despite the report's clear sentiment in this regard, its benchmarks are often so general as to make ascertaining their attainment dependent on MDBs' affirmations that recommended changes are being implemented. Of course, as the Task Force discovered, it is difficult to spell out precise performance criteria for every recommended change given the diversity and complexity of country and agency circumstances. We believe that the MDBs are probably unreformable largely because of that problem.

Third, the call for more public scrutiny and openness is consistent with the Task Force's overall efforts to deal with problems before or as they develop. Even for those who believe that the MDBs do have a role to play in international development, it is difficult to defend the publicly funded institutions' tradition of secrecy.

Although those three themes represent steps in the right direction, the most troublesome aspects of the report are its recommendations for continued or possible expansion of MDB activities in other areas, especially those related to the private sector and MDB promotion of free-market policies. The report does a fair job of suggesting that MDBs end their outdated traditional lending priorities, but it does not adequately justify other MDB missions in a changed world.

Financial Support for Private Projects

Private capital flows now dwarf official aid flows to the developing world. The report correctly notes that those flows and market-oriented development strategies suggest a declining relative role for the MDBs. The report nevertheless raises concerns about the fact that only about a dozen developing countries receive the bulk of that private capital. Yet that is precisely as it should be. Nations that have done the most to reform have succeeded in attracting voluntary, private money, while those that have been unwilling to change—as is the case for most sub-Saharan states—have not succeeded in doing so. The ability to attract capital is determined by the types of policies and institutions a country embraces.

Despite that evidence, some Task Force members desire an increased MDB role in guaranteeing or lending directly to private-sector projects. Indeed, recognition of the private sector as the source of wealth creation is usually cited to justify that type of MDB activity. But if the goal of the MDBs is to promote market economies, subsidizing or publicly guaranteeing private investment schemes is an inauspicious way of promoting the free market. Worse, such a move presents moral hazard problems. Official support for the private sector relieves host governments of the need to adopt an investment environment that would genuinely attract foreign capital. In the worst-case scenario, overreliance on such guarantees—which are determined not by market considerations alone but also by political considerations—could lead to a renewed developing-country debt problem. That is not at all an unthinkable outcome.

Policy-Based Lending

The report also notes that the MDBs' record of policy-based lending is poor. Structural adjustment loans, for example, have done little to change the policies of recipient nations and in practice have actually encouraged governments to maintain poor economic policies. As one Task Force member observed, "Ultimately the need to lend will overcome the need to ensure that those [loan] conditions are indeed met." Again, aid intended to advance market liberalization takes the pressure off recipient governments and allows them to postpone, rather than promote, necessary reforms. The free-market revolution that has swept much of the developing world since the fall of the Berlin Wall has been due to economic reality, not to years of policy-based lending during which development planning prevailed.

Because of the misuse of fast-disbursing lending to facilitate policy reform, the report recommends that MDBs be much more selective in making such loans. Unfortunately, the report does not explain why policy-based lending is necessary, other than to mention that the goals are desirable. The report also does not resolve the central problem that the MDBs face: their institutional incentive to continue lending.

The MDBs, after all, are in the awkward position of trying to discourage bad policy and encourage policy change through loan cutoffs and at the same time trying to encourage policy change through the release of more aid if a country promises to change policy. Yet releasing that aid would once again jeopardize reforms. Not releasing that aid, on the other hand, would mean that policy change would occur without MDB aid and thus run the risk that the MDBs would be viewed as irrelevant. The MDBs simply cannot afford to let developing countries reform on their own. In practice, the suspension and resumption of policy-based loans amounts to a "time-consuming and expensive ritual dance" between the MDB and the borrower government. As long as policy-based lending continues (even at the lower relative levels the report recommends), that problem will not be resolved. In short, we are in favor of market-oriented policy reform, but not in favor of MDB aid to supposedly promote market-oriented policy reform.

Poverty Reduction and Microenterprise Lending

The report recognizes that poverty reduction depends heavily on poor people's ability to use assets productively. Microenterprise institutions are cited as economically viable and particularly effective in empowering the world's poor. Indeed, many microenterprise banks appear to be highly successful, claiming to provide hundreds of millions of dollars in loans at market interest rates with repayment records better than those of commercial banks. Given those qualities, it is not clear why the MDBs should provide microfinance agencies subsidies or "seed capital" as called for by the report.

Microenterprise programs may alleviate the conditions of the poor, but they do not address the causes of the lack of credit faced by the poor. In developing countries, about 70 percent of poor people's property is not recognized by the state. Without secure property rights, the ability of the poor to create wealth (for example, by using collateral to obtain a loan or insure a small business) is severely limited. Without a doubt, the most important social program in the developing world would be the recognition and respect of poor people's property by the state. Of course, the scarcity of credit is also caused by a host of other policy measures such as financial regulations that make banking services prohibitively expensive for the poor.

Microenterprise lending can be beneficial, but successful programs need not receive aid subsidies. The success of those programs, moreover, will depend on specific conditions that vary greatly from country to country. For that reason, microenterprise projects should be financed privately by people with their own money at stake, rather than by the aid bureaucracies that appear intent on replicating such projects throughout the developing world.

Institutional Development

The private sector's proven ability to finance and operate development projects traditionally undertaken by governments has led some observers to suggest that MDBs move away from financing such projects and concentrate on technical assistance in setting up regulatory frameworks and agencies to oversee environmental or safety matters, for example. The Task Force report makes such a recommendation. It does not, however, suggest what model—U.S., Western European, or Japanese—the MDBs should impose on developing countries. Given the crisis of the regulatory welfare state in the developed world, such a recommendation does not appear particularly prudent. That is especially so given that the public debate, at least in the United States, has revolved around the question of whether such national regulatory agencies should continue to exist. The report provides little guidance about the appropriate level of regulation or alternatives to the regulatory state. Moreover, tasks such as judicial or educational reform are infinitely more complex than the relatively simple physical infrastructure projects in which the MDBs have developed a poor track record. Clearly, legal, environmental, safety, and other issues are important; but we are not at all confident in the MDBs' ability to provide the kinds of advice that will most benefit developing countries.

Natural Resources and Sustainable Development

The report makes reference to the "rapid increase in the use of natural resources" and the need for "conservation" and other regulatory measures to accomplish sustainable development. Unmentioned are the facts that the material standard of living as measured by most human development indicators has improved dramatically in the developing world in the past several decades and that the prices of virtually all natural resources have continued their long-term declines, which indicates their greater availability, not their scarcity.

We believe that a discussion of natural resources in this context is only meaningful if it takes into account how they relate to human welfare instead of simply measuring their absolute levels as indicators of present or future well-being. If, for example, humanity develops a way to use a given resource twice as efficiently as in the past, then, in terms of what it means for humanity, that resource has become relatively more abundant. The best way to ensure that resources continue to become more abundant and human welfare continues to improve is through the free-market price system, which incorporates a vast amount of ever-changing information dispersed throughout the world—something that regulators or central planners could not possibly achieve.

If, on the other hand, the static view of natural resources predominates, we believe that the regulatory framework that it requires will undermine the signaling function of the price system and thus hold down living standards, especially of the world's poor. Emphasis on regulation and government ownership of natural resources rather than on a private-property-rights regime will tend to be environmentally detrimental as well. In our view, what matters are the institutions— property rights, rule of law, freedom of exchange—not the absolute levels of the world's resources. The MDBs are thus not appropriate vehicles for promoting those institutions, particularly since the MDBs are inclined to provide regulatory solutions to environmental issues. Moreover, their own poor record on environmental matters, which has arisen largely because of their frequent disregard for human and private-property rights, provides little reason to believe that they can or should be in charge of implementing "environmental agendas" as the report recommends.

Conclusion

The Task Force report is useful in that it highlights the many problems associated with MDB lending and proposes reductions in many MDB activities. Nevertheless, it recommends a continued role for the MDBs that we believe is not adequately justified in the report. Indeed, to expand MDB activities in the areas mentioned above would be especially wrong headed. Moreover, we are dubious about further efforts at bureaucratic reform and believe that MDB problems go beyond the practical. In our opinion, the MDBs' development approach is fundamentally flawed in that it continues to view official outside aid and advice as essential for economic growth. The experiences of nations throughout world history contradict that view.

The report suggests that the MDBs are becoming less relevant in a changed world. In truth, the MDBs' irrelevance is merely becoming more evident. The United States should stop funding the MDBs and encourage the other industrialized states to do likewise. Together, they should promote international development by allowing as much commercial and other forms of peaceful interchange between their own private citizens and the rest of the world as possible.

James Sheehan has asked to be associated with these comments.

Statement by Senator Joseph R. Biden[75]

CSIS has performed a valuable service with the publication of *The United States and the Multilateral Development Banks*. It should mark the beginning of a serious debate on the role of these important institutions in our changing global economy.

As increasing trade and financial transactions weave a tighter web of economic relationships around the globe, we must be sure that our thinking and our institutions keep pace.

This report provides a thorough review of all aspects the Banks' operations, offers specific recommendations for improvements, and suggests criteria for judging the Banks' progress in meeting new standards for a new international economic environment.

Appropriately, the report maintains that our country's foreign policy priorities —not limited to strictly economic interests—require the continued viability and vitality of the Multilateral Development Banks.

Still, even the most dedicated friends of the Banks understand that they must grow and evolve to meet new circumstances. Around the world today, governments and private economic actors are adjusting to the disciplines and opportunities of the new international economy. The Banks can do no less.

In fact, many of the reforms recommended in this report have already been put into practice, demonstrating both the need for reforms highlighted in this report and the Banks' willingness to confront the need for change.

But there is more to be done to open the Banks' operations to the light of public participation—and public understanding—in both the donor nations who provide the capital resources and in the recipient nations where those resources are spent. And there must be greater assurance for the United States and its fellow donor countries that our foreign policy interests and principles are actively promoted by the Banks.

Our finite financial resources must be invested in ways that have the greatest chance of providing the greatest benefit for the most people. Indeed, that is why we created the Banks, and that can be the only justification for our continued participation.

In many ways, the Banks have justified the investment of our nation's money and international reputation that we have provided them over the years. It is now

---

75. Senator Biden became Ranking Minority Member on the Senate Foreign Relations Committee in January 1997; he was not a member of the Task Force but asked that this statement be included.

fitting that we review their practices, procedures and performance to assure that our participation will continue to be useful.

This report will help to set the agenda for that review.